MILITARY AND VETERAN ISSUES

U.S. MILITARY MEDICAL PROFESSIONALS

ETHICAL GUIDELINES, PRACTICES, AND ISSUES

MILITARY AND VETERAN ISSUES

Additional books in this series can be found on Nova's website under the Series tab.

Additional e-books in this series can be found on Nova's website under the e-book tab.

MILITARY AND VETERAN ISSUES

U.S. MILITARY MEDICAL PROFESSIONALS

ETHICAL GUIDELINES, PRACTICES, AND ISSUES

ERIN ANDREWS
EDITOR

New York

Copyright © 2016 by Nova Science Publishers, Inc.

All rights reserved. No part of this book may be reproduced, stored in a retrieval system or transmitted in any form or by any means: electronic, electrostatic, magnetic, tape, mechanical photocopying, recording or otherwise without the written permission of the Publisher.

We have partnered with Copyright Clearance Center to make it easy for you to obtain permissions to reuse content from this publication. Simply navigate to this publication's page on Nova's website and locate the "Get Permission" button below the title description. This button is linked directly to the title's permission page on copyright.com. Alternatively, you can visit copyright.com and search by title, ISBN, or ISSN.

For further questions about using the service on copyright.com, please contact:
Copyright Clearance Center
Phone: +1-(978) 750-8400   Fax: +1-(978) 750-4470   E-mail: info@copyright.com

NOTICE TO THE READER

The Publisher has taken reasonable care in the preparation of this book, but makes no expressed or implied warranty of any kind and assumes no responsibility for any errors or omissions. No liability is assumed for incidental or consequential damages in connection with or arising out of information contained in this book. The Publisher shall not be liable for any special, consequential, or exemplary damages resulting, in whole or in part, from the readers' use of, or reliance upon, this material. Any parts of this book based on government reports are so indicated and copyright is claimed for those parts to the extent applicable to compilations of such works.

Independent verification should be sought for any data, advice or recommendations contained in this book. In addition, no responsibility is assumed by the publisher for any injury and/or damage to persons or property arising from any methods, products, instructions, ideas or otherwise contained in this publication.

This publication is designed to provide accurate and authoritative information with regard to the subject matter covered herein. It is sold with the clear understanding that the Publisher is not engaged in rendering legal or any other professional services. If legal or any other expert assistance is required, the services of a competent person should be sought. FROM A DECLARATION OF PARTICIPANTS JOINTLY ADOPTED BY A COMMITTEE OF THE AMERICAN BAR ASSOCIATION AND A COMMITTEE OF PUBLISHERS.

Additional color graphics may be available in the e-book version of this book.

Library of Congress Cataloging-in-Publication Data

ISBN: 978-1-63484-697-4

Published by Nova Science Publishers, Inc. † New York

Contents

Preface vii

Chapter 1 Ethical Guidelines and Practices for
U.S. Military Medical Professionals 1
Defense Health Board

Chapter 2 A Proposed Ethic for Military Medicine 109
Thomas E. Beam and Edmund G. Howe

Index 135

Preface

Military health care professionals serve in a variety of settings, more diverse than is typically found in the civilian environment. The Military Health System (MHS) is a global, comprehensive, integrated system that includes combat medical services, peacetime health care delivery to Service members and eligible beneficiaries, public health services, medical education and training, and medical research and development. MHS personnel provide a continuum of health services from austere operational environments through remote, fixed military treatment facilities (MTFs), to major tertiary care medical centers distributed across the United States. Military health care professionals are also expected to care for detainees, enemy combatants, nonstate actors, local nationals, and coalition forces. In addition, U.S. military personnel are often deployed to assist in humanitarian missions, such as natural disasters or to provide care to local citizens in combat zones. Directly applying ethical principles from civilian medical ethics may not be appropriate in military medicine. The basic discrepancy between the two settings involves their goals and how these goals can be achieved. This book examines the ethical guidelines, practices, and issues for U.S. military medical professionals.

In: U.S. Military Medical Professionals
Editor: Erin Andrews

ISBN: 978-1-63484-697-4
© 2016 Nova Science Publishers, Inc.

Chapter 1

ETHICAL GUIDELINES AND PRACTICES FOR U.S. MILITARY MEDICAL PROFESSIONALS[*]

Defense Health Board

OFFICE OF THE ASSISTANT SECRETARY OF DEFENSE HEALTH AFFAIRS

March 3, 2015

MEMORANDUM FOR ASSISTANT SECRETARY OF DEFENSE FOR HEALTH AFFAIRS

SUBJECT: Ethical Guidelines and Practices for U.S. Military Medical Professionals Report

The Defense Health Board (DHB) is pleased to submit its report summarizing the findings and recommendations from our independent review on Ethical Guidelines and Practices for U.S. Military Medical Professionals, attached.

On January 29, 2013, the Acting Under Secretary of Defense for Personnel and Readiness endorsed a memorandum from the Assistant Secretary of Defense for Health Affairs (ASD(HA)) dated May 25, 2011, requesting the Defense Health Board (DHB) review military medical

---

[*] This is an edited, reformatted and augmented version of a report issued March 3, 2015.

professional practice policies and guidelines and report its findings to the ASD(HA). The DHB was specifically requested to provide responses to the following questions:

- How can military medical professionals most appropriately balance their obligations to their patients against their obligations as military officers to help commanders maintain military readiness?
- How much latitude should military medical professionals be given to refuse participation in medical procedures or request excusal from military operations with which they have ethical reservations or disagreement?

The DHB tasked its Medical Ethics Subcommittee to conduct its review of military medical professional practice policies and guidelines. The Subcommittee reviewed current civilian and military health care medical professional practice policies and guidelines as well as medical ethics education and training in the Department of Defense (DoD) and civilian institutions. Subcommittee members also held panel discussions with subject matter experts and DoD personnel, including Active Duty, National Guard, Reserve, and retired military health care medical professionals and line officers.

On behalf of the DHB, I appreciate the opportunity to provide DoD with this independent review of military medical professional practice policies and guidelines.

Nancy W. Dickey, M.D.
President, Defense Health Board

Attachments:
As stated
cc: USD(P&R)

EXECUTIVE SUMMARY

Military health care professionals serve in a variety of settings, more diverse than is typically found in the civilian environment. The Military Health System (MHS) is a global, comprehensive, integrated system that includes combat medical services, peacetime health care delivery to Service members and eligible beneficiaries, public health services, medical education and training, and medical research and development. MHS personnel provide a continuum of health services from austere operational environments through remote, fixed military treatment facilities (MTFs), to major tertiary care medical centers distributed across the United States. Military health care professionals are also expected to care for detainees, enemy combatants, nonstate actors, local nationals, and coalition forces. In addition, U.S. military personnel are often deployed to assist in humanitarian missions, such as natural disasters or to provide care to local citizens in combat zones.

In all settings, military and civilian, health care professionals face innumerable conflicts in the practice of their vocation. They might face inner conflicts over the morality or appropriateness of certain medical procedures at the beginning or end of life. They might face conflicts over the best use of scarce resources. Conflicting roles and expectations of how one fills multiple responsibilities and obligations can place the health care professional in a difficult and ambiguous situation. Potential ethical conflicts between professional standards and other values, commitments, or interests can become even more acute when health care professionals work in military environments.

At times, health care professionals who practice in these settings may face ethical challenges in honoring the ethical standards of their profession and obeying military orders or policies. For the military health care professional, it can be more pronounced in the combat or detainee setting. As a health care provider, the professional is obligated to preserve life, attend the sick and wounded, and minimize suffering, even on behalf of the enemy. On the other hand, the health care professional, as a Service member, is obligated to support the mission, maintain military readiness, and support military operations.

Tensions can arise if the demands of the mission or line command are at odds or in tension with the duties to attend to the health of those needing care. Military leadership is hierarchical and relies on formal authorities and chain of command. Decisions often have to be made quickly and decisively. This type of decision-making structure can be challenging to health care professionals who are facing ambiguous or uncharted territory that requires them to rely on their judgment, discretion, and in accordance with nonmilitary professional standards.

In particular, military personnel serving in combat zones might be confronted with numerous ethical and moral challenges. Most of these can be resolved with effective communication, training, leadership, clear rules of engagement, and unit cohesion and support. However, the very act of experiencing, witnessing, or participating in troubling events can undermine a Service member's humanity. An act of serious transgression that leads to serious inner conflict because the experience is at odds with core ethical and moral beliefs is called moral injury, which can be long lasting and painful.

Charge to the Defense Health Board

On January 29, 2013, the Acting Under Secretary of Defense for Personnel and Readiness endorsed a memorandum from the Assistant Secretary of Defense for Health Affairs (ASD(HA)) dated May 25, 2011, requesting the Defense Health Board (DHB) review military medical professional practice policies and guidelines and report its findings to the ASD(HA). "There are unique challenges faced by military medical professionals in their dual-hatted positions as a military officer and a medical provider. Such positions require them to balance and prioritize their role as an officer in the military and their role as a medical professional with ethical responsibilities to their patients. The following two questions from the ASD(HA) need to be reviewed and addressed by the Board:

- How can military medical professionals most appropriately balance their obligations to their patients against their obligations as military officers to help commanders maintain military readiness?
- How much latitude should military medical professionals be given to refuse participation in medical procedures or request excusal from military operations with which they have ethical reservations or disagreement?"

Methods and Scope of the Response

In response to this request, DHB tasked the Medical Ethics Subcommittee to conduct the review (see the Terms of Reference at Appendix B). Although the questions focused initially on medical officers, the Subcommittee agreed to expand the scope to all personnel who might be providing health care in military operations. Nurses, psychologists, psychiatrists, medics, other allied health professionals, and lower ranking personnel (collectively referred to as health care professionals) could also experience conflicting obligations, especially with regard to their rank in the chain of command. In addition, the

Subcommittee elected to focus primarily on the unique challenges faced by military health care professionals, while acknowledging the ethical dilemmas that all health care professionals—civilian and military—might face in the course of delivering care. Thus, its review and deliberations centered on situations that might be encountered regarding military readiness and operations in specific settings, for example, predeployment in garrison, deployed in a combat operation (i.e., battlefield to battalion aid station, forward surgical team, combat surgical or theater hospital), at a military detainee installation, or as part of a humanitarian mission.

The Medical Ethics Subcommittee reviewed current civilian and military health care professional practice policies and guidelines as well as medical ethics education and training within the Department of Defense (DoD) and civilian institutions. Members also conducted interviews with and received briefings from subject matter experts and DoD personnel including Active Duty, National Guard, Reserve, and retired military health care professionals and line officers. The members also spoke with individuals from the Uniformed Services University of the Health Sciences (USUHS). The members reviewed the literature and information received from briefings, conducted site visits, and presented their preliminary findings and recommendations to the DHB for consideration and deliberation.

The Subcommittee recognized that much has been written about military medical ethics[1-7] and it did not aim to reproduce or repeat much of the work that already has been done and published in this area. Rather it familiarized itself with the various ethical frameworks employed to consider ethical dilemmas faced by military health care professionals.

Finally, the Subcommittee developed its own principles to guide its review and deliberation on these issues (see Box A).

Box A. Guiding Principles

Context

Military health care professionals face unique challenges resulting from their dual role as medical providers and military personnel. Throughout their careers, these professionals may be required to plan and participate in health care support for combat operations, humanitarian assistance, disaster response and other activities, which may be conducted in austere environments with limited resources. As health care providers, military medical professionals have ethical responsibilities to their patients, which arise from a variety of legal, moral, and professional codes as well as personal moral and religious beliefs of both the caregiver and the patient. However, military health care professionals must weigh and prioritize these ethical responsibilities with their role as military officers.

The Guiding Principles provided herein guide the DHB and the Medical Ethics Subcommittee in its review of the dual loyalties of military health care professionals.

Overarching Principle:
DoD has a duty to provide military health care professionals with the resources, tools, and knowledge to determine the best course of action when confronted with ethical dilemmas and a practice environment in which they feel safe in raising ethical concerns and confident they will receive support in seeking a fair and just resolution to those concerns. In addition, DoD also has an obligation to assist professionals in developing the resiliency to cope with and recover from the moral injury resulting from confronting intractable ethical dilemmas.

Guiding Principles:
The recommendations provided by the DHB, when taken as a whole, must:

i. Take into consideration:

a. The spectrum of health care professional ethical codes, laws, and licensing requirements;
b. Military professional ethics and codes;
c. Medical education and continuing medical education both within and outside of DoD,
d. The spectrum of experiences of both civilian and military health care professionals;
e. The need for military health care professionals to explore and address their own and their patient's religious beliefs, ethics, and medical preferences; and
f. Recommendations of those within and outside of DoD.

ii. Provide guidance regarding how to best educate and train military health care professionals to recognize and determine the best course of action when ethical dilemmas arise.

> iii. Acknowledge the moral injury that may occur as a result of encountering an ethical dilemma and incorporate practices that enhance resiliency and assist professionals in coping with and recovering from these injuries.
> iv. Provide guidance to ensure a support infrastructure and environment is established and maintained to provide military health care professionals a safe avenue to raise ethical concerns and seek timely assistance in determining the best courses of action.

Response to the Charge

Below is a summary of key aspects of the responses to the two questions posed by the ASD(HA) in the request for this report.

> How can military medical professionals most appropriately balance their obligations to their patients against their obligations as military officers to help commanders maintain military readiness?

As described in this report, military health care professionals can rely on ethics guidance and standards developed by their professional societies to guide difficult ethical decisions. These codes provide a solid foundation on which to base ethical decision making, and the elements described in the codes are remarkably consistent across the professions. In addition, DoD and Military Department policies, instructions, manuals, and standard operating procedures provide comprehensive and often detailed procedural guidance that implicitly operationalize many of the ethical principles expressed in professional codes.

Further, the Subcommittee found that *a priori* education and training provide the best strategies for providing military health care professionals with the skills, experience, and knowledge they can draw on when confronting difficult ethical choices. Consideration of plausible scenarios, combined with knowledge of existing codes of ethics and DoD policies, plus the opportunity to discuss the relevant issues *before* being in the heat of a situation will provide health care professionals with the working knowledge needed to make the best choice possible, given the circumstances. DoD must ensure that such education and training is available and that resources are available on an ongoing basis for personnel to seek help and information online or though consultations. Following deployment, DoD must provide means for health care professionals to acknowledge and resolve moral injuries that they might have experienced during deployment.

How much latitude should military medical professionals be given to refuse participation in medical procedures or request excusal from military operations with which they have ethical reservations or disagreement?

Most organizations representing health care professionals have a code of medical ethics by which members of that profession are expected to adhere, including processes for resolving conflict. State medical boards have standards of professional conduct that must be maintained as a condition of licensure. Many State laws also permit health care professionals to invoke a conscience clause by which they may refuse to perform a legal role or responsibility based on moral or other personal objections.

The Subcommittee notes that if the operation is illegal, every military member of every specialty has an obligation to do all in his or her power to stop it or refuse participation.

If a medical procedure is immoral or unethical according to the standards of the health care professional's belief system, then the senior medical officer should seek another similarly qualified professional to replace the individual who objects to the procedure.

If a medical procedure is considered unethical according to any of the various systems that apply, then concerned parties need to resolve the conflict as time and circumstances allow before proceeding with an action. If resolution is not possible, opposing views should be given to the commander who must make the final decision regarding military operational readiness. Conflicts should be resolved through the medical chain of authority or military chain of command or both.

DoD leadership, particularly the line commands, should excuse health care professionals from performing medical procedures that violate their professional code of ethics, State medical board standards of conduct, or the core tenets of their religious or moral beliefs. However, to maintain morale and discipline, this excusal should not result in an individual being relieved from participating in hardship duty. Additionally, health care professionals should not be excused from military operations for which they have ethical reservations when their primary role is to care for the military members participating in those operations.

The Need for a Systems Approach to Military Medical Ethics Preparation and Practice

Throughout the history of the United States, all branches of the military have continually endeavored to develop and abide by honorable and ethical standards and principles in the preparation for and conduct of war. Over the past decade, DoD has taken action in response to concerns regarding ethical issues to improve its policies and training. Oversight, conduct, and training for detainee operations have improved. Scenarios involving challenging ethical decisions have been incorporated into pre-deployment training exercises. Ethical principles have been emphasized in professional development courses for enlisted, non-commissioned officers, and officers. However, there is room for improvement, as suggested by the recommendations provided in this report.

Finding 1

DoD has many efforts already underway to promote ethical conduct in the military health care setting. However, DoD does not have a formal, integrated infrastructure to promote an evolving ethical culture within the military health care environment. Creating a comprehensive ethics infrastructure within the MHS could foster and inform ethical conduct in health care and could serve to lessen, mitigate, or assist in resolving ethical conflicts that might arise among health care professionals or between health care professionals and line leadership.

Recommendation 1

DoD should further develop and expand the infrastructure needed to promote DoD-wide medical ethics knowledge and an ethical culture among military health care professionals, to include: a code of ethics; education and training programs; consultative and online services; ethics experts; and an office dedicated to ethics leadership, policy, and oversight. To achieve these goals, DoD should form a tri-Service working group with appropriate representation to formulate policy recommendations on medical ethics. This should include development of a DoD Instruction to guide development of the infrastructure needed to support the ethical conduct of health care professionals. In addition, this working group should consider the best ways to implement the recommendations in this report.

Medical Ethics

Ethical standards are an important part of professional practice in medicine, law, engineering, science, accounting, military service, and other professions. They establish expected norms of behavior that help members of the profession work toward common goals and promote the public's trust in the profession. These obligations are over and above the moral obligations that apply to all members of society.

Ethics in health care is guided by a set of principles that apply across a wide range of settings. Most discussions of medical ethics focus on a core set of ethical principles, specifically autonomy, beneficence, nonmaleficence, and justice. Numerous professional health care associations have guidelines or codes of ethics or conduct for their members that incorporate these ethical principles, and regularly update them in response to economic and financial shifts in the health care environment, social transformation, technological advances, and changing patient demographics. In addition, State medical boards have standards of professional conduct that must be maintained as a condition of licensure. Such codes, guidelines, and standards provide tenets or principles for professional conduct and are developed through a consensus of the relevant constituency and oversight body, if relevant. They universally require complete loyalty to patients. Professional codes are often intended to transcend legal, policy, or regulatory requirements. They not only address the ethical principles that should be adhered to when caring for patients but they also establish standards for how professionals should and should not conduct themselves. Several professional organizations also include in their ethics codes statement about the health care professional's role in interrogation and torture, care of detainees, and treatment of hunger strikers.

In an ideal setting, several mechanisms are in place to assist health care professionals with difficult ethical choices. For example: 1) they can invoke conscience clauses if they refuse to perform a legal role or responsibility based on moral or other personal objections; 2) they can seek an ethics consultation in which a trained clinical ethicist serves as a consultant to a member of a health care team, a patient, or a family member. These options might not always be available in the military setting.

Finding 2

The Subcommittee reviewed the ethics codes of multiple health care professional organizations, as well as the management of ethics consultations in health care settings. Existing codes are consistent with and applicable to much of the health care practiced by military personnel in the MHS. All emphasize the health care professional's primary responsibility to the patient. However, unique challenges can arise when there are real or perceived conflicts among professional codes of conduct, personal values, patient values, and requirements of the chain of command.

Recommendation 2
Throughout its policies, guidance, and instructions, DoD must ensure that the military health care professional's first ethical obligation is to the patient.

Finding 3
Most organizations representing health care professionals have a code of medical ethics by which members of that profession are expected to adhere. State medical boards have standards of professional conduct that must be maintained as a condition of licensure. Many State laws also permit health care professionals to invoke a conscience clause by which they may refuse to perform a legal role or responsibility based on moral or other personal objections.

Recommendation 3
DoD leadership, particularly the line commands, should excuse health care professionals from performing medical procedures that violate their professional code of ethics, State medical board standards of conduct, or the core tenets of their religious or moral beliefs. However, to maintain morale and discipline, this excusal should not result in an individual being relieved from participating in hardship duty. Additionally, health care professionals should not be excused from military operations for which they have ethical reservations when their primary role is to care for the military members participating in those operations.

Finding 4
DoD does not have an explicit code of ethics for health care professionals.

Recommendation 4
DoD should formulate an overarching code of military medical ethics based on accepted codes from various health care professions to serve as a guidepost to promote ethical leadership and set a standard for the cultural ethos of the MHS. To inform this process, the ethics codes of relevant health

care professional organizations should be reviewed regularly and updates should be made to the military medical ethics code as appropriate.

Finding 5

DoD has not issued directives or instructions regarding the organization, composition, training, or operation of medical ethics committees or medical ethics consultation services within the MHS. It is not clear that consistent, high quality ethical consultation services are readily available to military health care professionals and it may be less likely that deployed units have such specialized expertise available to them, at least not in an organized fashion.

Recommendation 5

To provide formal ethics guidance, direction, and support to the MHS and its components, DoD and the Military Departments should:

a) Publish directives/instructions regarding the organization, composition, training and operation of medical ethics committees and medical ethics consultation services within the MHS. DoD should review best practices at leading civilian institutions in formulating this guidance.
b) Ensure military treatment facilities have access to consistent, high-quality, ethical consultation services, including designation of a responsible medical ethics expert for each location. For those facilities/locations without onsite medical ethics support, DoD should ensure remote consultation is available.
c) Provide a "reach back" mechanism for deployed health care professionals to contact an appropriately qualified individual to assist in resolving an ethical concern that has not been resolved through their chain of command.
d) Develop a small cadre of clinicians with graduate level training in bioethics to serve as senior military medical ethics consultants.
e) Ensure that health care professionals are knowledgeable about their rights and available procedures for obtaining ethics consultation, expressing dissent or requesting recusal from certain objectionable procedures or activities.
f) Review compliance with ethics directives and instructions as part of recurring health service inspections.

Principles and Practice of Military Ethics

Military ethics are centered on an established culture of high standards, values, and personal conduct. Ethical virtues, including loyalty, duty, respect, selfless service, honor, integrity, and personal courage, are ingrained into the military ethos. Loyalty and obedience are integral to much that has been written about military values and ethics. The concept of loyalty requires that the individual subordinate personal interests to the requirements of military duty. To be loyal requires integrity; that is, putting duty before personal interests. It also might require reporting infractions or ethical concerns. Integrity, loyalty, and honor also require that officers and commanders lead with an eye toward the efficiency of the unit, the mission, and the needs and welfare of one's subordinates. Pressures to honor these values can escalate in a combat setting or other austere environments. Combat stress can lead to altered perceptions of "what is right." Leadership can mitigate stress and a breakdown in moral values by ensuring that the mission is ethically valid, that leadership understands and supports the need of subordinates, and that options are available whenever possible for subordinates to access the help of chaplains or mental health professionals in times of personal conflict.

Numerous DoD and Military Department policies and rules dictate how military values are to be operationalized generally and in specific settings and contexts including stabilization or humanitarian missions and detainee installations. Military health care professionals must adhere to these requirements as well as additional mandates specific to health care and the health care environment. International law and rules of engagement also apply.

The Subcommittee reviewed DoD policies and guidance regarding standards of conduct, ethics regulations, and related training requirements. It also reviewed DoD policy specific to health care professionals, such a medical handbooks and manuals, health service support in humanitarian mission, disaster relief, and stabilization operations. Instructions targeted to health care professionals were reviewed, including response to sexual assault, protection of private health information, medical program support for detainee operations, medical treatment of hunger strikers, and international policies such as the Geneva Conventions. Although extensive guidance, instruction, and doctrine have been issued relevant to the expectations and responsibilities of health care professionals in a variety of military contexts, there are some areas where guidance might be confusing or not readily accessible in a timely way, as discussed below.

Ethical Issues in Military Medical Settings

While military health care professionals face all of the same ethical dilemmas found in the civilian health care sector, they can face even more within the context of military medicine. In garrison or in theater they might face difficult requests by the command to provide information about the health status of a Service member. In the combat or austere environment, challenging ethical decisions concerning, for example triage, often have to be made by relatively junior professionals. These physicians and other health care professionals might be tasked with responsibilities for which they were not specifically trained. Additionally, they might have only received a few weeks' notice of deployment, and, if in the National Guard or Reserve Component, might be leaving behind a civilian job and responsibilities to patients, peers, and institutions at home. They are not likely to have trained with their unit or been the beneficiaries of advance training that involves extensive briefings or field exercises. Once deployed, they might work under dual chains of command, the line and the medical officer.

Fitness for Duty Examinations and Screening: Disclosure to the Command

Military health care professionals described challenges in responding to commanders who sometimes requested more information on a patient's health status than may be appropriate or necessary. Patient concerns regarding release of information to leadership can alter the therapeutic relationship between providers and their patients and lead some Service members to withhold certain information or seek care in the civilian sector. In contrast, if a Service member discusses personal health concerns or psychological health problems with a chaplain, the chaplain has special privileges that protect him or her from being ordered or asked to breach the Service member's privacy. With increased concerns regarding both suicide prevention and ensuring patients are not a danger to themselves, others, or the mission, significant pressure has been placed on some health care professionals to provide more information to more elements of leadership than may ordinarily seem appropriate.

Finding 6

Military health care professionals report a lack of clarity in policies regarding the level of detail that should routinely be provided to commanders regarding a military member's health status and treatment. Without clear guidance, each provider has to determine whether there is potential for impact, and each might have a different threshold for disclosure.

Recommendation 6

DoD should develop clear guidance on what private health information can be communicated by health care professionals to leadership, and the justifications for exceptions to the rule for reasons of military necessity.

Finding 7

Lawyers and Chaplains are afforded unique status and privileges with respect to the confidential relationships they have with military personnel seeking their services.

Recommendation 7

DoD should provide military health care professionals with privileges similar to those of Chaplains and Judge Advocates regarding their independence and obligation to protect privacy and confidentiality while meeting the requirements of line commanders.

Treatment Priorities or Triage for Casualties in the Military Setting

The battlefield is a particularly challenging setting in which to provide health care. Demands on resources can create conflict. Fatigue and constant stress can impede clear thinking. Health care professionals might not have the time to consider and weigh all options. One of the most difficult ethical situations in the heat of battle can be in setting treatment priorities and triage for casualties. The complexity and possibility for resulting moral injury on the part of the health care professional tasked with making difficult choices about scarce resources also suggest that some sort of debriefing process, either during or after deployment, be in place to help these professionals work through and justify difficult ethical decisions made under duress. Post-deployment debriefing is discussed further below.

Humanitarian Assistance, Disaster Response, and Medical Support Missions

The U.S. military has a long tradition of providing humanitarian relief after war or natural disaster. In recent years, the U.S. military is increasingly providing medical support for U.S. forces, coalition forces, and civilian populations in a broad range of missions including peace operations, humanitarian assistance, disaster relief, and nation assistance. In other circumstances, U.S. personnel are mentoring host nation health care providers; that is, not actually providing care, but serving as medical advisors.

These missions can raise unique and different challenges for health care professionals that differ from those found in military operations, for example, wide variations in medical assets and practices among coalition members and variability in medical readiness among coalition forces. Differences in standards of care and medical practice from country to country can pose ethical dilemmas for health care professionals. Yet health care professionals have an obligation to help with urgent medical problems and will have an understandable desire to respond to medical need, regardless of the official mission.

Finding 8

Cultural norms, social expectations, and rules of engagement can create unique challenges for those providing care to non-U.S. personnel or serving as medical mentors to developing world host nation personnel. Providing care in the context of humanitarian assistance or disaster relief operations may involve unique stressors in coping with extensive unmet health care needs with limited resources. Health care professionals would benefit from having a thorough understanding of the issues associated with these operations including the underlying cultural beliefs, social expectations, resource limitations, and altered treatment priorities associated with these environments.

Recommendation 8

DoD should provide specific education and training for health care professionals designated to serve as medical mentors or health care providers in foreign health care facilities or in support of humanitarian assistance or disaster relief operations. Such education and training should cover cultural differences, potential ethical issues, rules of engagement, and actions that might be taken to avert, report, and address unethical, criminal, or negligent behavior or practices.

Detainee Installations

Detainee installations can provide unique challenges for health care professionals who are required to provide routine health care to detainees, assess the ability of detainees to undergo lawful forms of interrogation, accurately report health status in medical records, and respond to hunger strikes, some of which can be prolonged. The ethical codes of health care professional groups universally condemn the involvement of their members in any form of physical or psychological abuse. Evolving DoD policy and guidance has clarified the responsibilities of health care professionals in such settings.

Deployments and Professional Support

Like any Service member, military health care professionals face uncertainty throughout their careers in terms of postings, relocations, and deployments. National Guard and Reserve Component personnel face the prospect of last minute assignments and deployments that take them away from their civilian employment and community. Deployments to combat zones can be intense and stressful. The ways in which medical officers train and deploy can exacerbate the potential for future issues. Insufficient opportunity to debrief after returning from deployment may also be a missed opportunity to prevent or mitigate moral injury in some individuals or groups.

In addition, health care professionals cannot always resolve ethical conflicts alone even if there is unit cohesion. Resources and support are needed for addressing conflicts and raising an issue up the medical chain of command. If appropriate communication and training occurs, the likelihood of conflict or the desire to recuse oneself from certain actions is less likely to occur. However, when it does, institutional support, policies, and a culture must be in place to allow individuals with legitimate concerns to express and act on them. When institutional ethics go awry, individuals must feel empowered as moral agents to report problems and challenge the institution. They must have ready access to policies and instructions that can guide their decision making. The Subcommittee heard from medical officers that line commanders are not always fully aware of the special codes of conduct and ethical principles to which health care professionals must adhere.

Finding 9

DoD does not have an online portal to provide efficient access to medical ethics information and resources.

Recommendation 9

DoD should create an online medical ethics portal. At a minimum, it should include links to relevant policies, guidance, laws, education, training, professional codes, and military consultants in medical ethics.

Finding 10

It is not evident that line leadership always has a clear understanding of the roles, responsibilities, and limitations of health care professionals with respect to what actions they may or may not take and what information they may or may not provide based on ethical codes, licensure standards of conduct, and legal restrictions.

Recommendation 10

DoD should include in professional military education courses information on the legal and ethical limitations on health care professionals regarding patient care actions they may or may not take in supporting military operations and patient information they may and may not communicate to line leadership.

Post-Deployment Issues

Post-deployment, health care professionals indicated to the Subcommittee that having an opportunity to debrief, particularly following deployments that involved intensely emotional experiences, may be of benefit in coping with any moral injury and reducing the sense of isolation. It also provides an opportunity to identify those who need additional help. In addition, health care professionals usually deploy from active positions at MTFs. As such, other members of the medical team must compensate for the individual who has left on a deployment, taking on additional patients and responsibilities. This situation can lead to additional stress when the Service member is expected to return directly to work upon their return, where there might be little empathy or support for what the individual might have encountered while deployed. These demands of the MTF could prevent the Service member from properly debriefing and reintegrating back into life in garrison while coming to terms with any challenging situations experienced while deployed.

Finding 11

Military health care professionals could benefit from opportunities for debriefing, particularly following deployments that involved intensely emotional experiences, as a means of coping with moral injury and reducing their sense of isolation. Debriefing may also provide an opportunity to identify those who need additional help post-deployment.

Recommendation 11

DoD should ensure that systems and processes are in place for debriefing health care professionals to help them transition home following deployment. Debriefing should occur as a team when possible. Not only could this help mitigate potential moral injury in health care professionals, but it may also provide lessons learned and case studies for inclusion in ongoing training programs.

Finding 12

Having senior medical officers as full members of the Commander's staff provides an opportunity for regular two-way communication. Medical leaders would have insight to key goals, issues, and concerns of the command while also ensuring that the Commander is aware of medical limitations and potential ethical concerns in planning and operations.

Recommendation 12

To create an environment that promotes ethical conduct and minimizes conflicts of dual loyalty, DoD leadership should emphasize that senior military health care professionals are full members of the Commander's staff as an advisor on medical ethics as it relates to military readiness.

Ethics Education and Training

Military health care professionals receive ethics guidance in the form of both formal education and military training. One noteworthy source of military specific ethics education for health care professionals is USUHS. However, most military health care professionals have not attended USUHS, joining the military after receiving education in the civilian sector. These individuals receive some level of traditional medical ethics instruction through their formal education and receive military ethics guidance through subsequent military training. The level, intensity, and nature of ethics education is likely to vary based on the specific civilian institution. However, outside of annual ethics training regarding behavior relevant to finances and relationships with contractors, ethics training has been described as limited and inconsistent across the Military Departments.

In addition to formal education, continuing education programs offer a variety of ethics courses to military health care professionals. While these and other medical ethics courses are not part of a formalized and required curriculum, many state health care licensing bodies do require specific continuing education hours in ethics. As military health care professionals maintain state issued licenses, such courses may be an individual requirement.

As mentioned previously, some active duty Service members who are health care professionals described challenges in deploying as individuals, without the opportunity to train or bond with their unit prior to deployment. As ethical training opportunities reported by Service members varied greatly, deploying as individuals could lead to a wide range of ethical training in a particular unit. Some Service members also noted that by simply filling in on deployments as an individual and not training with their unit, they miss the opportunity to build trust with the rest of the unit. This lack of trust could influence an individual's ability to evaluate complex ethical situations with other members of their unit.

Finding 13

When Service members simply fill in slots on deployments as an individual and do not train with their unit, they miss an opportunity through the training environment to establish relationships and build trust with members of their unit prior to deployment. This could make resolution of medical ethical conflicts that occur more challenging in the deployed environment.

Recommendation 13

To minimize isolation of health care professionals, the Military Departments should make every effort to ensure personnel who are deploying to the same location train together as a team prior to deployment. Establishing relationships prior to deployment may enable better communication and trust among line command and health care professionals in the deployed setting.

Finding 14

Medical ethics education and training appear to vary among Military Departments and specialties. DoD would benefit from having a common baseline education and training requirement in medical ethics across the Military Departments to ensure a consistent understanding and approach to medical ethics challenges.

Recommendation 14

DoD should issue a directive or instruction designating minimum requirements for basic and continuing education and training in military medical ethics for all health care professionals in all components and indicate the appropriate times in career progression that these should occur.

Finding 15

In recognition that health care professionals will come from different education and training backgrounds, personnel preparing for deployment would benefit from a pre-deployment review of key ethics challenges, reminders of available support tools and information, and provision of contact information for resources that might be of assistance should an ethical challenge rise. Health care professionals indicated that including challenging medical ethics scenarios in realistic pre-deployment and periodic training was beneficial for both line and medical personnel.

Recommendation 15

To enhance ethics training for military health care professionals and the line command, DoD should:

a) Ensure pre-deployment and periodic field training includes challenging medical ethics scenarios and reminders of available resources and contact information to prepare both health care professionals and line personnel. Curricula should include simulations and case studies in addition to didactics.

b) Provide a mechanism to ensure scenarios and training curricula are continually updated to reflect specific challenges and lessons learned through debriefing from real-world deployments and garrison operations.

c) Ensure key personnel returning from deployment who have faced significant challenges provide feedback to assist personnel preparing for deployment.

Finding 16

Joint Knowledge Online provides a Basic and Advanced Course in Medical Ethics and Detainee Health Care Operations. These courses provide valuable information for deploying health care professionals on ethical issues related to the care of detainees.

The current implementation of the course could be improved to provide more efficient communication of the concepts and scenarios covered. In addition, it would be beneficial to have a course covering basic principles of medical ethics for all health care professionals.

Recommendation 16

To enhance health care practices in the military operational environment, DoD should:

a) Update the Joint Knowledge Online Medical Ethics and Detainee Health Care Operations courses to improve the efficiency with which the information is communicated and maintain currency of the material.
b) Create a medical ethics course to cover key principles, ethical codes, and case studies applicable to both garrison and deployed environments, in addition to providing resources and appropriate steps to take when assistance is needed in resolving complex ethical issues. This course should be required for all health care professionals.

About This Report

The next section provides a brief introduction to the report. **Section 2** describes the principles and practice of medical ethics. In addition to discussing the various ethical frameworks that one might rely on to develop principles for ethical practice, the section summarizes how these principles are codified in the standards and oaths of many national and international medical professional groups and how principles are operationalized through ethics committees and consultations. Recommendations are made to facilitate ethical conduct of health care professionals.

Section 3 describes the principles and practice of military ethics, focusing on a review of existing doctrine and guidance (in the form of DoD Instructions, Directives, and Manuals) that operationalize relevant military and health care ethical principles.

Section 4 discusses the ethical issues that might arise specific to military settings as a means to understanding how existing guidance and doctrine can be used to guide actions or might require review or revision.

Section 5 describes existing DoD ethics education and training programs and makes recommendations for improvement.

The **final section** presents the Subcommittee's perspective on creating an enterprise-wide systems approach to military medical ethics preparation and practice.

1. Introduction

"I, ____, having been appointed an officer in the Army of the United States, as indicated above in the grade of ____ do solemnly swear (or affirm) that I will support and defend the Constitution of the United States against all enemies, foreign and domestic; that I will bear true faith and allegiance to the same; that I take this obligation freely, without any mental reservation or purpose of evasion; and that I will well and faithfully discharge the duties of the office upon which I am about to enter; So help me God." (Department of the Army Form 71, July 1999, for officers)."[†][8]

"I will apply, for the benefit of the sick, all measures which are required, avoiding those twin traps of overtreatment and therapeutic nihilism."

Modern Hippocratic Oath, in part.

Primum non nocere ("first, do no harm")

Ethical standards are an important part of professional practice in medicine, law, engineering, science, accounting, military service, and other professions. Ethical standards establish expected norms of behavior that help members of the profession to work toward common goals and promote the public's trust in the profession. While the various professions share some core values, their ethical standards differ somewhat, depending on their goals.[9] Professional ethical standards are special obligations that individuals undertake when they enter a profession. These obligations are over and above the moral obligations that apply to all members of society. For example, medical professionals have a duty to promote human health that extends far beyond the obligation that all people have to help others. Medical professionals are often required to place their own health or life at risk to promote the health of their patients.

There are two important barriers in any organization to violating societal ethical norms – the individual and the ethical infrastructure of the organization. The individual's ethos is the last resort to exposing or stopping unethical behavior in an organization. However, the most important factor for

---

[†] While this is the Officer Oath specific to the Army, the main body of the oath is similar between all the Military Departments. Additionally, officers may choose between "affirm" and "swear" and are not required to state "so help me God."

an organization is having an infrastructure promoting ethical leadership and an ethical cultural ethos.[10,11] The prevalence of unethical behavior is diminished when an organization has an ethical infrastructure that promotes these objectives.

Military ethics are centered on an established culture of high standards for personal conduct. Ethical virtues, including loyalty, duty, respect, selfless service, honor, integrity, and personal courage, are ingrained into the military ethos. These ethical standards are applicable to all who serve, including health care professionals, who also are expected to adhere to the ethical standards of their profession.[12] Military professionals are often required to place their own health or life at risk in service to their nation or its interests. Although military professionals are expected to follow orders they have been given under the chain of command, they must sometimes exercise their independent ethical judgment when faced with an order they believe to be unlawful or immoral.

Health care ethics focuses on promoting the best interests of the patient while respecting his or her autonomy and confidentiality. Members of different health care professions, for example, medicine, nursing, and pharmacy, have developed professional codes and guidelines that embody the virtues of loyalty to the patient, compassion, justice, safety, and professional integrity and excellence.[13] Although health care professionals often work for organizations (such as hospitals) that require them to follow certain policies or rules, they also exercise their independent, ethical judgment when deciding how to act.

In all settings, health care professionals face innumerable conflicts in the practice of their vocation.[13] They might face inner conflicts over the morality or appropriateness of certain medical procedures at the beginning or end of life. They might face conflicts over the best use of scarce resources, for example, vaccines or drugs in short supply. Conflicts can arise when there are competing demands on their time by employers or payers or when a patient's family expresses preference for a treatment course that might not be in the best interest of the patient. When the science of medicine is imprecise or evolving, conflict can arise about the most appropriate treatment plan for a patient given an array of expert opinions about what is best. At times, a health care professional might feel conflicted by the need to breach the confidentiality of a patient in order to better protect the patient or others, for example, in the case of abuse or in the event of a public health emergency. Finally, conflicting roles and expectations of how one fills multiple responsibilities and obligations can place the health care professional in a difficult and ambiguous situation. Against this backdrop of numerous potential conflicts, medical ethics has long urged the health care professional to be, first and foremost, loyal to the people in their care.[14-17] That obligation can be difficult to meet when other obligations compete for priority.

Potential ethical conflicts between professional standards and other values, commitments, or interests can become even more acute when health care professionals work in military environments. Health care professionals who practice in these settings may have to choose between honoring the ethical standards of their profession and obeying military orders or policies. Difficulties related to dealing with these conflicting ethical obligations may cause those who work in military health care moral distress and may result in longterm moral injury.[18] Processes and procedures should be implemented in the military environment to help health care professionals deal with conflicting ethical obligations.

1.1. Distinctive Considerations in Military Settings

The concept of dual loyalty, sometimes called mixed agency, refers to circumstances in which a professional might feel a duty or loyalty to more than one cause, authority, or agent.[19] For the military health care professional, it can be more pronounced in the combat or detainee setting.[20-23] As a health care provider, the professional is obligated to preserve life, attend the sick and wounded, and minimize suffering, even on behalf of the enemy. On the other hand, the health care professional, as a Service member, is obligated to support the mission, maintain military readiness, and support military operations. Health care professionals are authorized to use arms in their own defense or in defense of the patients in their care.[24] Tensions can arise if the demands of the mission or line command are at odds or in tension with the duties to attend to the health of those needing care. Military leadership is hierarchical and relies on formal authorities and chain of command. Decisions often have to be made quickly and decisively. This type of decision-making structure can be challenging to health care professionals who are facing ambiguous or uncharted territory that requires them to rely on their judgment and discretion and act in accordance with nonmilitary professional standards.

Although military health care professionals face the same types of conflicts and tensions that any provider faces in the civilian setting, several additional factors may arise in military settings, particularly in the pre-deployment or deployed combat environment or in military detainee installations. In addition, military health care professionals are often first on the scene to provide humanitarian aid in the event of a natural or man-made disaster where they might be working with teams from other nations who adhere to different standards and obligations. Examples of situations where tensions can arise include the following:

- Experiencing pressures to clear individuals for deployment or redeployment;
- Establishing treatment or triage priorities for casualties;
- Coping with scarce resources or environments that result in substandard care or inability to care for certain nonmilitary populations;
- Providing care in the face of fatigue, stress, and threats to personal safety;
- Administering unproven treatments with or without the consent of the patient;
- Being asked to assist in interrogations;
- Being asked to care for a detainee's health, including force feeding;
- Working across cultural and language differences;
- Returning Service members to combat (preserving unit effectiveness).

In each of these cases, the military health care professional could experience real or perceived conflicts between their role as a member of the Armed Forces and their obligations as a health care provider (see Section 2 for a discussion of obligations). If they feel strongly that what is being required of them violates their personal or professional ethical commitments, they might refuse participation in health care procedures or request excusal from military operations. Such actions could put them in conflict with their obligations as Service members.

The special role played by health care professionals on the battlefield and in military operations has long been recognized, with international humanitarian law forbidding combatants from interfering with or thwarting the efforts of medical personnel. Of note, this level of protection has not been honored in recent conflicts; for example, there have been repeated attacks on Fallujah General Hospital in Iraq. In addition, the nature of warfare has changed, further complicating the medical decision-making environment. Medical professionals might find themselves in environments of volatility, uncertainty, complexity, and ambiguity, in which traditional roles and expectations are blurred because of the nature of the combatant forces. They also could be treating civilian populations that do not share similar values. For example, they might be asked to delay or forgo treatment of women and children until the men in a village are treated. It is inevitable that such conflicts will continue to arise in the future. Thus, the focus for the Department of Defense (DoD) should be on developing strategies to manage and mitigate them.

1.2. The Need for a Systems Approach to Military Medical Ethics Preparation and Practice

Throughout the history of the United States, all branches of the military have continually endeavored to develop and abide by honorable and ethical standards and principles in the preparation for and conduct of war. Over the past decade, DoD has taken action in response to concerns regarding ethical issues to improve its policies and training. Oversight, conduct, and training for detainee operations have improved. Scenarios involving challenging ethical decisions have been incorporated into pre-deployment training exercises. Ethical principles have been emphasized in professional development courses for enlisted, non-commissioned officers, and officers. However, there is room for improvement, as suggested by the recommendations provided in this report.

Finding 1

DoD has many efforts already underway to promote ethical conduct in the military health care setting. However, DoD does not have a formal, integrated infrastructure to promote an evolving ethical culture within the military health care environment. Creating a comprehensive ethics infrastructure within the Military Health System could foster and inform ethical conduct in health care and could serve to lessen, mitigate, or assist in resolving ethical conflicts that might arise among health care professionals or between health care professionals and line leadership.

Recommendation 1

DoD should further develop and expand the infrastructure needed to promote DoD-wide medical ethics knowledge and an ethical culture among military health care professionals, to include: a code of ethics; education and training programs; consultative and online services; ethics experts; and an office dedicated to ethics leadership, policy, and oversight. To achieve these goals, DoD should form a tri-Service working group with appropriate representation to formulate policy recommendations on medical ethics. This should include development of a DoD Instruction to guide development of the infrastructure needed to support the ethical conduct of health care professionals. In addition, this working group should consider the best ways to implement the recommendations in this report.

2. PRINCIPLES AND PRACTICE OF MEDICAL ETHICS

"Medical ethics in times of armed conflicts is identical to medical ethics in times of peace."[25]

World Medical Association

Ethics in health care is guided by a set of principles that apply across a wide range of settings. The field of medical ethics has evolved and expanded over time. Its earliest broadly known manifestation was in the Hippocratic Oath, which was the standard for the ethical conduct of physicians for centuries. Medical ethics emerged as a widely acknowledged discipline in the mid-20th century as technological advances provided physicians and other health care professionals with new and transformative possibilities to save lives, such as transplanting organs, treating infertility, and furthering controversial areas of research. These opportunities also posed difficult questions for the health care community, for example, "who should receive scarce and vital treatment (such as organs)?"; "how should society determine when life ends?"; "what restrictions if any should be placed on care for the dying?"; and "should health care professionals be required to provide services that they find morally objectionable (e.g., abortion)?"[26] Today the field of medical ethics focuses broadly on discussions of what society should do with regard to the care of patients as well as what individual practitioners should do in their own health care practice.

"Organizational ethics" pertains to the ethical policies, procedures, and values of an organization.[27] Organizational ethics is important in health care, scientific research, business, military operations, and other settings where people share a common work environment and goals. One of the most important considerations in organizational ethics is to promote an ethical culture in the organization. An ethical culture is one in which members of the organization understand the importance of following ethical standards, they are familiar with the ethical standards of the organization, and they have the resources to deal with ethical dilemmas, issues, and problems. To promote an ethical culture, organizational leaders should develop and publicize ethics policies and procedures, support ethics education and consultation, and implement systems for overseeing conduct and reporting unethical or illegal activities. Leadership is also important for promoting an ethical culture, since unethical leadership can lead to ethical indifference and corruption. Leaders should set a moral example for members of the organization and stress the importance of ethics in their communications and decisions.

The term "clinical ethics," first discussed by Joseph F. Fletcher in *Morals and Medicine*,[28] refers specifically to the ethical challenges that arise in the care of patients, that is, the moral choices that must be made in the day-to-day health care setting. It is sometimes case-specific and considers technical, legal, and ethical issues.[29] The field of clinical ethics gave rise to the practice of ethics consultation and the use of ethics committees (described further below).

"Research ethics" has always been a field distinct from medical ethics, although related in many ways, and is a subset of the broader field of bioethics. It emerged as a field largely in response to the Nazi atrocities involving experimentation on prisoners without their consent and the subsequent issuance of the Nuremberg Code, and later the Declaration of Helsinki.[30] Research ethics extends beyond the protection of human subjects in research and includes the ethics of animal research, data management, authorship, collaboration, publication, and other topics. It also considers the implications of emerging areas of science and whether limits should be in place for these emerging areas, such as human cloning, synthetic biology, or recombinant DNA research. Ethical standards apply to investigators conducting clinical research on patients as well as scientists conducting basic research in the laboratory. Scientific research, like clinical medicine, is usually overseen by ethics committees, such as Institutional Review Boards for human subjects research and Animal Care and Use Committees for animal research. Of note, there will be situations in which a clinician is also a researcher. For example, Section 3 describes a situation in which a decision was made out of military necessity to allow the use of investigational drugs or vaccines in Service members without adhering to the usual standards for informed consent.

However, this report focuses only on the clinical setting, recognizing that research ethics shares with medical ethics some basic principles (see Figure 1).

> The *Belmont Report*, written by the National Commission for the Protection of Human Subjects of Biomedical and Behavioral Research in 1978, was intended to serve as a guide for ethical human subjects' research. It established three principles for ethical research: respect for persons, beneficence, and justice. Respect for persons requires that autonomous individuals, that is, people who are capable for making competent choices, may participate in research only if they provide informed consent. Individuals who have diminished autonomy that interferes with their ability to consent can participate in research only if extra protections are in place to safeguard their welfare.[31] Beneficence requires that the risks of research are minimized and the benefits are maximized. Justice requires that the benefits and risks of research are distributed fairly. The Belmont principles are the basis of the current U.S. Federal Policy for the Protection of Human Subjects (or the Common Rule, codified by DoD at 32 CFR Part 219), which govern nearly all federally sponsored research, and all research supported or conducted by DoD.

From The National Commission for the Protection of Human Subject of Biomedical and Behavioral Research, 1978.[31]

Figure 1. Research Ethics.

This chapter briefly summarizes the basic theories and principles of medical ethics and describes how they are operationalized in a selected set of guidelines and codes of ethics of professional health care organizations and in ethics consultations and committees. (See Appendix D for a brief description of fundamental ethical theories.) It describes the Subcommittee's findings and provides recommendations for enhancing the Department of Defense's (DoD's) efforts to ensure a robust medical ethics environment.

2.1. Universal Medical Ethics Principles

Most discussions of medical ethics focus on a core set of ethical principles, as described below.[13] These principles can apply in more than one way. For example, autonomy could refer to the rights of patients or the rights of health care professionals. An advantage of ethical principles is that they tend to be less controversial and abstract than moral theories (see **Appendix D**).

Autonomy refers to the right of competent individuals to make informed decisions free from coercion or undue external influences. In the realm of health care, it typically relates to the informed consent process, in which a competent patient is informed of the risks and potential benefits of clinical procedures so he or she can decide whether to receive them.

However, in the context of practical medical ethics, autonomy of the health care provider might be invoked when conscientiously objecting to certain procedures or, in the military setting, refraining from following what one might consider to be immoral orders. Without question, it might be difficult at times to decide what makes an order immoral, but the meaning of this phrase may be a function of the individual's moral conscience and cultural factors. The autonomy of the military health care provider can also be more restricted than that of his or her counterpart in the civilian sector in that a civilian can choose not to work in a certain setting or for a particular employer.

Beneficence requires that health care professionals act in the patient's best interest, which is usually understood as promoting the patient's health. Beneficence may sometimes conflict with autonomy and one must decide how to balance these principles. For example, a patient might refuse certain lifesaving treatment because of religious objections or because he or she is terminally ill and wants to be allowed to die without additional burdensome interventions. There is an ethical consensus that in the civilian setting competent patients should be allowed to refuse medical treatment; however, military members may be reluctant to refuse treatment if refusal could affect their medical readiness for service. Beneficence may also conflict with justice in a military setting. For example, military medical triage might require treating the more minimally wounded before the more seriously wounded in order to return as many soldiers as possible to the battlefield. In this case, the health care professional might be compelled to make decisions that provide the greatest benefit for the greatest number, even if that could result in loss of benefit to a given patient.

Nonmaleficence requires that the health care professional do no harm or not impose unnecessary or unacceptable burdens on the patient. Nonmaleficence must often be balanced against beneficence because helpful medical treatments may also cause harm. For example, a drug used to treat arthritis may have undesirable side effects, such as gastrointestinal bleeding or distress. Health care professionals must balance benefits and risks when deciding what is in the patient's best interests. The principle of nonmaleficence is invoked in codes that prohibit health care professionals' involvement in, for example, execution, torture, or interrogations. (See discussion below.)

Justice includes a formal principle and material principles. The formal principle requires that similar cases be treated similarly. Material principles determine what makes cases similar or different. For example, if one adopts medical need as a material principle, then patients with the same medical needs should receive the same treatment. The term *distributive justice* refers to a societal obligation to distribute benefits, resources, risks, and costs fairly. Triage procedures are a type of distributive justice. Military medical ethics sometimes confronts the challenge of treating similar patients similarly. If health care professionals are compelled to treat all like patients in the same way—whether they are U.S. personnel, civilians, or enemy combatants—some would argue that this would imply that enemy combatants or civilians might receive treatment at the expense of large numbers of military personnel, which could challenge the mission and decrease morale.[32]

2.2. The Concept of Moral Injury

Military personnel serving in combat zones will be confronted with numerous ethical and moral challenges. Most of these can be resolved with effective communication, training, leadership, clear rules of engagement, and unit cohesion and support. However, the very act of experiencing, witnessing, or participating in troubling events can undermine a Service member's humanity. "Transgressions can arise from individual acts of commission or omission, the behavior of others, or by bearing witness to intense human suffering or the grotesque aftermath of battle. An act of serious transgression that leads to serious inner conflict because the experience is at odds with core ethical and moral beliefs is called *moral injury*."[33]

Litz et al have defined moral injury as "perpetrating, failing to prevent, bearing witness to, or learning about acts that transgress deeply held moral beliefs and expectations."[34] The concept suggests that individuals "who struggle with transgressions of moral, spiritual, or religious beliefs are haunted by dissonance and internal conflicts. In this framework, harmful beliefs and attributions cause guilt, shame, and self-condemnation." Recognized as a significant consequence of war, research is focused on how best to provide "moral repair and renewal;" that is, developing methods for facilitating recovering of a Service member's sense of humanity. These approaches can include psychological or emotional processing of the memory of the moral transgression, its meaning and significance, and the implication for the Service member, or exposure to corrective life experiences.[34] (See further discussion in Section 4 on approaches to moral repair [moral resilience/courage] post-deployment.)

2.3. Professional Codes of Ethics and Standards of Ethical Conduct

Numerous professional health care associations have guidelines or codes of ethics or conduct for their members that incorporate the ethical principles described above and regularly update them in response to economic and financial shifts in the health care environment, social transformation, technological advances, and changing patient demographics. In addition, State medical boards have standards of professional conduct that must be maintained as a condition of licensure. Such codes, guidelines, and standards provide tenets or principles for professional conduct and are developed through a consensus of the relevant constituency and oversight body, if relevant. In general, they all focus on the principles of autonomy, beneficence, nonmaleficence, confidentiality (the obligation to safeguard confidential medical information), and justice. They universally require complete loyalty to patients. However, there are circumstances in which absolute loyalty to a patient can be justifiably challenged (see Figure 2).

> There are examples in health care in which absolute loyalty to a patient might be trumped by concerns for the greater public good:
>
> In both the military and civilian settings, a health care professional may be required, by law, to breach patient confidentiality to protect a third party from a significant and imminent threat of harm or to notify public health or law enforcement officials of a communicable diseases, physical abuse, or violence.
>
> In some cases, a Service member may be required to receive treatment for an infectious disease, such as tuberculosis, even if he or she refuses treatment, in order to protect the health of his or her unit.
>
> In both the military and civilian settings, a patient with an infectious disease may be quarantined against his or her will in order to protect public health and the other members of the unit.

Figure 2. Examples of Exceptions to Absolute Loyalty to a Patient.

Professional codes are often intended to transcend legal, policy, or regulatory requirements (see Section 3). They not only address the ethical principles that should be adhered to when caring for patients but they also establish standards for how professionals should and should not conduct themselves. What follows are excerpts from a sampling of these codes that are of particular relevance to this review.

The Hippocratic Oath asserts that the physician must act to benefit his or her patient and protect confidentiality. It also requires that the physician use the resources of society for the benefit of the individual. It was an inherently paternalistic framework in that it made no mention of the patient's right to choose and asserted that the physician was in the best position to decide what's best for the patient.[35] In contrast, the current "Principles of Medical Ethics" of the American Medical Association (AMA) require that the physician respect the rights of patients, colleagues, and other health professionals.[36]

The AMA's guidelines focus on the physician's obligation to respect patients and alleviate suffering, citing the principles of beneficence and nonmaleficence, confidentiality, professional independence, and respect for autonomy (the patient as person). The AMA's *Declaration of Professional Responsibility* states that the physician must, among other things:

> Respect human life and the dignity of every individual.
> Refrain from supporting or committing crimes against humanity and condemn all such acts.
> Treat the sick and injured with competence and compassion and without prejudice.[37]

The American Psychiatric Association adheres to the *Principles of Medical Ethics* of the AMA with some annotations specifically applicable to psychiatry.[38]

The American Nurses Association's (ANA's) *Code of Ethics for Nurses with Interpretive Statements* also emphasizes duty to the patient: "The nurse's primary commitment is to the patient, whether an individual, family, group, community or population."[16(p.5)]

The American Psychological Association cites the additional principles of fidelity and responsibility of psychologists, that is, the duty to establish relationships of trust and the need to be aware of professional and scientific responsibilities to society and the profession.[39]

Many guidelines have statements about how to resolve conflicts. For example, the code of the American Psychological Association states:

> If the demands of an organization with which psychologists are affiliated or for whom they are working are in conflict with this Ethics Code, psychologists clarify the nature of the conflict, make known their commitment to the Ethics Code, and to the extent feasible, resolve the conflict in a way that permits adherence to the Ethics Code . . . Under no circumstances may this standard be used to justify or defend violating human rights.[39(p.15)]

Similarly, the American Academy of Physician Assistants (AAPA) instructs its members to use its guidelines when facing an ethical dilemma or to seek guidance from "a supervising physician, a hospital ethics committee, an ethicist, a trusted colleague, or other AAPA policies."[40(p.3)]

The ANA's code urges nurses to consider patients first when resolving conflicts of interest, stating:

> Nurses must examine the conflicts arising between their own personal and professional values, the values and interests of others who are also responsible for patient care and healthcare decisions, and perhaps even the values and interests of the patients themselves. Nurses address such conflicts in ways that ensure patient safety and that promote the patient's best interests while preserving the professional integrity of the nurse and supporting interprofessional collaboration.[16(p.5)]

Some codes specifically address the autonomy of the health care provider. For example, AMA's *Principles of Medical Ethics* state, "A physician shall, in the provision of appropriate patient care, except in emergencies, be free to choose whom to serve, with whom to associate, and the environment in which to provide medical care."[36]

Likewise, the American Osteopathic Association's *Code of Ethics* addresses the autonomy of physician's choices in providing care:

> The physician must have complete freedom to choose patients whom she/he will serve. However, the physician should not refuse to accept patients for reasons of discrimination, including, but not limited to the patient's race, creed, color, sex, national origin, sexual orientation, gender identity or handicap. In emergencies, a physician should make her/his services available.

A physician is never justified in abandoning a patient. The physician shall give due notice to a patient or to those responsible for the patient's care when she/he withdraws from the case so that another physician may be engaged.

In any dispute between or among physicians involving ethical or organizational matters the matter in controversy should first be referred to the appropriate arbitrating bodies of the profession.[41]

The World Medical Association's (WMA's) *Regulations in Times of Armed Conflict and Other Situations of Violence* focus specifically on duties during battle, stating "Medical ethics in times of armed conflicts is identical to medical ethics in times of peace."[25]

During times of armed conflict and other situations of violence, standard ethical norms apply, not only in regard to treatment but also to all other interventions, such as research.

The medical duty to treat people with humanity and respect applies to all patients. The physician must always give the necessary care impartially and without discrimination on the basis of age, disease or disability, creed, ethnic origin, gender, nationality, political affiliation, race, sexual orientation, or social standing or any other similar criterion.

Whatever the context, medical confidentiality must be preserved by the physician. However, in armed conflict or other situations of violence, and in peacetime, there may be circumstances in which a patient poses a significant risk to other people and physicians will need to weigh their obligation to the patient against their obligation to other individuals threatened.

In emergencies, physicians are required to render immediate attention to the best of their ability. Whether civilian or combatant, the sick and wounded must receive promptly the care they need. No distinction shall be made between patients except those based upon clinical need.[25]

Another recurring theme in professional codes is the need to protect the privacy or confidentiality of patients. Federal statutes such as the Health Insurance Portability and Accountability Act Privacy Rule also bind all health care providers to protect individually identifiable health information that is transmitted or maintained in any form or medium. Individual States also have statutes governing the confidentiality of patient and client information, the protection of data gathered in research, and the privacy of students. In the military setting, breaches of confidentiality or privacy can affect a Service member's status in terms of promotions, placements, and deployments.

Guidelines for ethical conduct are not restricted to professional organizations. Of interest, the U.S. Department of Health and Human Services' Agency for Healthcare Research and Quality has issued guidelines for health care providers responding to mass casualty situations in *Mass Medical Care with Scarce Resources: A Community Planning Guide*.[42] The agency refers to "ethical preparedness," stating, "Sound planning can take this expectation into account by providing ethical guidelines and principles for making tough choices in a real-time environment."[42(p. 12)] Specifically, the guidance highlights: Focus on Consequences (the greatest good for the greatest number); Focus on Duties and Obligations; Rights and Fairness; and Respect Community Norms.

Statements on Interrogation and Torture

The WMA's Declaration of Tokyo - Guidelines for Physicians Concerning Torture and other Cruel, Inhuman or Degrading Treatment or Punishment in Relation to Detention and Imprisonment prohibits any form of medical participation in interrogation, even if the practices and methods comply with the law. The Declaration states, "the physician shall not use nor allow to be used, as far as he or she can, medical knowledge or skills, or health information specific to individuals, to facilitate or otherwise aid any interrogation, legal or illegal, of those individuals."[43] It further states, "The physician shall not be present during any procedure during which torture or any other forms of cruel, inhuman or degrading treatment is used or threatened."

The International Dual Loyalty Working Group of Physicians for Human Rights includes in its guidelines: "The health professional is responsible for ensuring physical and mental health care (preventive and promotive) and treatment, including specialized care when necessary; ensuring follow-up care; and facilitating continuity of care— both inside and outside of the actual custodial setting— of convicted prisoners, prisoners awaiting trial, and detainees who are held without charge/trial."[44]

The AMA Code of Medical Ethics prohibits physicians' direct participation in interrogation.[45] Similarly, the American College of Physicians holds that it is unethical for a "...physician to be used as an instrument of government for the purpose of weakening the physical or mental resistance of another human being."[46] It has also clarified that "Physicians must not conduct, participate in, monitor, or be present at interrogations, or participate in developing or evaluating interrogation strategies or techniques."[46]

In 2006, the American Psychiatric Association issued a policy statement against psychiatrists directly participating in interrogation.[47] Both the AMA and American Psychiatric Association permit physicians to train interrogators to recognize and respond to persons with mental illnesses and to understand possible medical and psychological effects of particular techniques and conditions of interrogation.

In 2013, the American Psychological Association revised and consolidated its policies related to the involvement of psychologists in military and national security interrogations. The 2013 policy also strengthened the APA position on torture stating: "Any direct or indirect participation in any act of torture or other forms of cruel, degrading or inhuman treatment or punishment by psychologists is strictly prohibited. There are no exceptions."[48]

Care of Detainees

A recent area of contention within the military medical community has focused on force feeding detainees who are hunger striking. With regard to detainees, the WMA
Declaration of Tokyo states:

> Where a prisoner refuses nourishment and is considered by the physician as capable of forming an unimpaired and rational judgment concerning the consequences of such a voluntary refusal of nourishment, he or she shall not be fed artificially. The decision as to the capacity of the prisoner to form such a judgment should be confirmed by at least one other independent physician. The consequences of the refusal of nourishment shall be explained by the physician to the prisoner.

The WMA has stated in its Declaration of Malta that force feeding is "never ethically acceptable" and "feeding accompanied by...coercion, force or use of physical restraints...is a form of inhuman and degrading treatment."

The ANA has been monitoring the force-feeding of detainees at Guantanamo Bay for approximately six years. In response to the case of a Navy medical officer (a registered nurse) who refused to continue managing tube-feedings of prison hunger strikers and was reassigned to "alternative duties," the ANA issued a statement supporting the right of the medical officer to refuse to perform such procedures. The statement and a letter to the Secretary of Defense urged "military leadership to recognize the ethical code of conduct to which professional registered nurses are accountable." The statement also advocated "for the establishment of a process within the uniformed services that allows for a thorough review of the type of situation and is receptive to concerns raised by the registered nurse who is compelled to question the plan of care."[49]

Although not a professional code, related to this, the U.S. Federal Bureau of Prisons has a policy for forced treatment of inmates who engage in hunger strikes under Title 28 of the Code of Federal Regulations, Part 549, Subpart E.[50] This policy states that following medical evaluation and management and after reasonable efforts to convince the inmate to accept treatment voluntarily, "or in an emergency preventing such efforts, a medical necessity for immediate treatment of a life or health threatening situation exists, the physician may order that treatment be administered without the consent of the inmate. Staff shall document their treatment efforts in the medical record of the inmate."[50] However, there are "significant differences" between the practices on force-feeding in Guantanamo Bay and the U.S. Federal Bureau of Prisons. The U.S. Federal Bureau of Prisons usually does not use a force-feeding restraining chair; it must report to a sentencing judge as to what it did, and the final authority in prisons is the physician.[51]

Conscience Clauses

Health care professionals can invoke conscience clauses if they refuse to perform a legal role or responsibility based on moral or other personal objections. The use of this clause largely focuses on reproductive health issues. Most states enacted such clauses after the 1973 *Roe v. Wade* decision legalizing abortion. More recently, pharmacists have invoked it in refusing to dispense emergency contraception.[52] Yet such clauses are to be invoked judiciously because they may interfere with the patient's best interests or autonomy. For example, in a formal opinion, the American College of Gynecologists and Obstetricians (ACOG) wrote:

> Personal conscience, so conceived, is not merely a source of potential conflict. Rather, it has a critical and useful place in the practice of medicine. In many cases, it can foster thoughtful, effective, and humane care. Ethical decision making in medicine often touches on individuals' deepest identity-conferring beliefs about the nature and meaning of creating and sustaining life. Yet, conscience also may conflict with professional and ethical standards and result in inefficiency, adverse outcomes, violation of patients' rights, and erosion of trust if, for

example, one's conscience limits the information or care provided to a patient. Finding a balance between respect for conscience and other important values is critical to the ethical practice of medicine.[53]

Because objections to providing care based on conscience affect someone's health or access to care, considerations must also be given to the patient's rights. Thus, codes of conduct recommend that health care professionals with moral objections to specific services alert their colleagues to these objections and that the conscientious objector not interfere with the patient's ability to obtain the services elsewhere. ACOG's opinion further states:

1) Physicians and other health care professionals have the duty to refer patients in a timely manner to other providers if they do not feel that they can in conscience provide the standard reproductive services that their patients request.
2) In an emergency in which referral is not possible or might negatively affect a patient's physical or mental health, providers have an obligation to provide medically indicated and requested care regardless of the provider's personal moral objections.
3) In resource-poor areas, access to safe and legal reproductive services should be maintained. Conscientious refusals that undermine access should raise significant caution. Providers with moral or religious objections should either practice in proximity to individuals who do not share their views or ensure that referral processes are in place so that patients have access to the service that the physician does not wish to provide. Rights to withdraw from caring for an individual should not be a pretext for interfering with patients' rights to health care services.[53(p 5-6)]

The ability of a patient to seek another provider in a timely manner can be challenging, particularly in an austere environment or where human resources are scarce.

2.4. Ethics Consultation and Ethics Committees

Ethics consultation, in which the principles of medical ethics are practiced in real-world situations, has become routine in the health care setting. A trained clinical ethicist serves as a consultant when called to service by a member of a health care team, a patient, or a family member. The consultant's role is to assess the facts relevant to the request, clarify the issues, explicate ethical values or principles, and provide a considered opinion, but not to make a decision for the person requesting the consultation.[54] The ethics consultant is obligated to inform the physician-in-charge that a consult has been requested. Ethics consults can be conducted by an individual or by a specially appointed institutional committee.

Ethics committees were created in response to some high-profile medical ethics controversies, in particular the Karen Anne Quinlan case in New Jersey in 1976. In that case, the New Jersey Supreme Court ruled that the dispute between the health care team and Karen Anne Quinlan's family about extraordinary measures to keep her alive should be referred to the hospital's ethics committee for clarification and advice.[55] In 1992, the role of these committees was formalized further when the Joint Commission (formerly the Joint Commission for the Accreditation of Health Care Organizations) recommended that health care organizations create some way of addressing ethical concerns.

The AMA provides guidelines for ethics consultations in its Opinion 9.115, stating, "Ethics consultations may be called to clarify ethical issues without reference to a particular case, facilitate discussion of an ethical dilemma in a particular case, or resolve an ethical dispute. The consultation mechanism may be through an ethics committee, a subset of the committee, individual consultants, or consultation teams."[56] The guidelines recommend, "All hospitals and other health care institutions should provide access to ethics consultation services. Health care facilities without ethics committees or consultation services should develop flexible, efficient mechanisms of ethics review that divide the burden of committee functioning among collaborating health care facilities."[56]

The American Society for Bioethics and Humanities (ASBH) describes the health care ethics (HCE) consultation as:

> "A set of services provided by an individual or group in response to questions from patients, families, surrogates, healthcare professionals, or other involved parties who seek to resolve uncertainty or conflict regarding value-laden concerns that emerge in health care. . . HCE consultants seek to identify and support the appropriate decision maker(s) and to promote ethically sound decision making by facilitating communication among key stakeholders, fostering understanding,

clarifying and analyzing ethical issues, and including justifications when recommendations are provided."[57]

The ASBH also states HCE consultants have an obligation "to be sufficiently informed about issues on which they communicate publicly, including an understanding of facts and scholarship relating to the topic."[57] The organization has issued core competencies for the HCE consultant.[58]

Questions have been raised about the effectiveness and use of ethics consultations. For example, although 95 percent of general hospitals surveyed in 1999 and 2000 offered ethics consultation or were starting up a consult service, these services handled an average of three cases a year.[59] Reasons for low use include concerns of health care professionals that their decisions will be undermined or that they would be subject to heightened legal scrutiny if a case were to come before such a review.[60,61] If individuals are given the consultant title with insufficient training or time as an extra duty, providers might not have confidence in the value of seeking their services.[61] Currently professionals in the field are considering the benefits and challenges of professionalizing the field through a certification process.[62] ASBH is developing qualifications for sitting for certification.

Of note, ASBH has issued its own code of ethics describing the core ethical responsibilities of individuals performing health care ethics consultation, to include:

1) Be competent.
2) Preserve integrity.
3) Manage conflicts of interest and obligation.
4) Respect privacy and maintain confidentiality.
5) Contribute to the field.
6) Communicate responsibly.
7) Promote just health care with HCEC [health care ethics consultation].[63]

Several high-profile and complex cases over the past decade have highlighted the need for expert assistance with difficult ethical challenges faced by providers in the military health care environment. The Joint Commission requires medical facilities to have a process that permits staff, patients, and families to address ethical issues. According to the 2014 DoD *Review of the Military Health System*, a large majority of military treatment facilities (MTFs) are accredited by The Joint Commission.[64] Thus, expectations are in place that MTFs have some system for addressing emerging ethical issues. Based on briefings provided to the Subcommittee, it is not clear that such services are readily available to military health care professionals and it is likely that deployed units may not have any such specialized expertise available to them, at least not in an organized fashion.

2.5. Ethics Consultations and Services at the Department of Veterans Affairs

The Department of Veterans Affairs (VA) has developed a program to address the need for ethics consultations across the Veterans Health Administration (VHA).[65] Its National Center for Ethics in Health Care serves as the department's authoritative resource for addressing the complex ethical issues that arise in patient care, health care management, and research. It provides information, education, and consultation and oversees nationwide programs and quality improvement projects for health care practitioners and administrators to understand and apply health care ethics standards. Through its national consultation service it responds to questions of health care ethics from VHA leaders and facility-based ethics program staff. However, VA recommends that Veterans, families, staff, and involved parties at field facilities seek consultation from their local VA medical center. Every VA medical center has an ethics consultation service.

2.6. Findings and Recommendations

Finding 2

The Subcommittee reviewed the ethics codes of multiple health care professional organizations, as well as the management of ethics consultations in health care settings. Existing codes are consistent with and applicable to much of the health care practiced by military personnel in the Military Health System (MHS). All emphasize the health care professional's primary responsibility to the patient. However, unique challenges can arise when there are real or perceived conflicts among professional codes of conduct, personal values, patient values, and requirements of the chain of command.

Recommendation 2

Throughout its policies, guidance, and instructions, DoD must ensure that the military health care professional's first ethical obligation is to the patient.

Finding 3

Most organizations representing health care professionals have a code of medical ethics by which members of that profession are expected to adhere. State medical boards have standards of professional conduct that must be maintained as a condition of licensure. Many State laws also permit health care professionals to invoke a conscience clause by which they may refuse to perform a legal role or responsibility based on moral or other personal objections.

Recommendation 3

DoD leadership, particularly the line commands, should excuse health care professionals from performing medical procedures that violate their professional code of ethics, State medical board standards of conduct, or the core tenets of their religious or moral beliefs. However, to maintain morale and discipline, this excusal should not result in an individual being relieved from participating in hardship duty. Additionally, health care professionals should not be excused from military operations for which they have ethical reservations when their primary role is to care for the military members participating in those operations.

Finding 4

DoD does not have an explicit code of ethics for health care professionals.

Recommendation 4

DoD should formulate an overarching code of military medical ethics based on accepted codes from various health care professions to serve as a guidepost to promote ethical leadership and set a standard for the cultural ethos of the MHS. To inform this process, the ethics codes of relevant health care professional organizations should be reviewed regularly and updates should be made to the military medical ethics code as appropriate.

Finding 5

DoD has not issued directives or instructions regarding the organization, composition, training, or operation of medical ethics committees or medical ethics consultation services within the MHS. It is not clear that consistent, high quality ethical consultation services are readily available to military health care professionals and it may be less likely that deployed units have such specialized expertise available to them, at least not in an organized fashion.

Recommendation 5

To provide formal ethics guidance, direction, and support to the MHS and its components, DoD and the Military Departments should:

a) Publish directives/instructions regarding the organization, composition, training and operation of medical ethics committees and medical ethics consultation services within the MHS. DoD should review best practices at leading civilian institutions in formulating this guidance.
b) Ensure military treatment facilities have access to consistent, high-quality, ethical consultation services, including designation of a responsible medical ethics expert for each location. For those facilities/locations without onsite medical ethics support, DoD should ensure remote consultation is available.
c) Provide a "reach back" mechanism for deployed health care professionals to contact an appropriately qualified individual to assist in resolving an ethical concern that has not been resolved through their chain of command.
d) Develop a small cadre of clinicians with graduate level training in bioethics to serve as senior military medical ethics consultants.
e) Ensure that health care professionals are knowledgeable about their rights and available procedures for obtaining ethics consultation, expressing dissent or requesting recusal from certain objectionable procedures or activities.
f) Review compliance with ethics directives and instructions as part of recurring health service inspections.

2.7. Conclusion

Just as a health care professional needs reliable sources of information for clinical issues that arise, he or she should also have resources for assistance when ethical challenges arise. Guidelines must be coupled with strategies to support health care professionals and counter the systemic forces that can erode both military and medical ethics and values.

Clear ethical guidelines, supplemented with law, can often clarify difficult ethical dilemmas in health care. When there are no clear or directly applicable laws or guidelines, health care professionals must be able to draw on their moral and ethical values, with professional codes and standards providing the foundation. This requires that military health care professionals receive comprehensive education and training in ethics to assist in decision making and to prepare for the potential challenges he or she could face. **Section 5** expands on the need for ethics education and training.

3. PRINCIPLES AND PRACTICE OF MILITARY ETHICS

3.1. Introduction: Core Military Values

Military ethics are centered on an established culture of high standards, values, and personal conduct. Ethical virtues, including loyalty, duty, respect, selfless service, honor, integrity, and personal courage, are ingrained into the military ethos (Figure 3). Historically, values and ethics of the military developed in concert with the role of the military in society.[66] From the influence of tradition and distinctive comradery of the Roman legionnaires to the chivalrous conduct of medieval knights to the large professional armies of the 19th century, military culture throughout history has developed "institutional expectations concerning the conduct and character of military professionals."[66(p. 131)]

U.S. Army Professional Values	U.S. Navy Core Values	U.S. Air Force Values
Loyalty	Honor	Integrity
Duty	Commitment	Service before self
Respect	Courage	Excellence
Selfless service		
Honor		
Integrity		
Personal courage		

Figure 3. Military Professional Values.

As described in depth in the Borden Institute *Military Medical Ethics* volumes on the evolution of military professionalism, despite centuries of military history, there is no formally published code of ethics for the military professional. Hartle writes that each Military Department has standards of conduct and all personnel are subject to the Uniform Code of Military Justice, which establishes military law.[66(p.141)] DoD and the Military Departments also issue guidance, instructions, and field manuals that serve as doctrinal counsel for the military professions (see below). Most relevant, DoD enforces a Code of Conduct (CoC) across the Military Departments. The CoC, established by Executive Order 10631 and as amended by Executive Orders 12017 and 12633, outlines basic responsibilities and obligations of members of the U.S. Armed Forces. All members of the Armed Forces are expected to meet the standards the CoC embodies.[67]

International law and rules of engagement also apply. Military personnel are sworn to uphold and defend the U.S. Constitution, which contains Article 6, Clause 2, requiring that international treaties signed by the United States Government be observed as the law of the land.

3.2. Military Codes of Ethics

The U.S. Armed Forces have many publications describing the ideals to which members are expected to aspire. Of these, the *Armed Forces Officer* provides the overarching guidance for the common moral-ethical grounding of all professional military officers,[68] just as *The Noncommissioned Officer and Petty Officer* does so for enlisted leaders.[69] The Center for the Army Profession and Ethic (CAPE) notes the omission of a formal articulation of an Army Ethic in U.S. Army doctrine, but states that it exists and emanates from the "heritage, beliefs, traditions, and culture" of the U.S. Army. CAPE proposes an Army Ethic and its guiding moral principles in a July 2014 white paper[70] and solicits feedback to achieve consensus on its expression. The proposal focuses on themes of honorable service, character, integrity, competence, commitment, and accountability. The U.S. Navy has published a "Navy Code of Ethics," which consists of a list of "Do" and "Do Not" statements.[71] These focus on themes of fraud, waste, abuse, citizenship, impartiality, and equal opportunity. The code of ethics for the U.S. Air Force is embodied in the publication "United States Air Force Core Values," which fully develops the meaning and application of these values.[72] DoD also references a "Military Code of Ethics" by referring to the codes of conduct in DoD Regulations 5500.7-R. Chapter 2, discussed below.[73]

3.3. Loyalty, Obedience, Unit Cohesion, and Subordination

Loyalty and obedience are integral to much that has been written about military values and ethics. The concept of loyalty requires that the individual "subordinate personal interests to the requirements of military duty."[66(p.144)] To be loyal requires integrity; that is, putting duty before personal interests. It also might require reporting infractions or ethical concerns. Kirkland writes that such reporting "helps to maintain the standards of the organization" and can serve to protect one's comrades.[74(p.161)] Integrity, loyalty, and honor also require that officers and commanders lead with an eye toward the efficiency of the unit, the mission, and the needs and welfare of one's subordinates. Pressures to honor these values can escalate in a combat setting or other austere environments. Kirkland writes that personnel in combat settings need a "credible and appropriate ethical foundation to sustain themselves psychologically."[74(p.178)] Combat stress can lead to altered perceptions of "what is right."

Leadership can mitigate stress and a breakdown in moral values by ensuring that the mission is ethically valid, that leadership understands and supports the need of subordinates, and that options are available whenever possible for subordinates to access the help of chaplains or mental health professionals in times of personal conflict.[74] With regard to access to Chaplains and the role of religion in Military commanders are responsible to provide for the free exercise of religion of those under their authority as directed by *Joint Publication (JP) 1, Doctrine for the Armed Forces of the United States*.[75]

Separate from the role of ethics, hierarchy and authority also play central roles in military culture. Given the nature of the military hierarchy, there is an understood lack of complete autonomy. Lawful orders established and dictated by leadership and higher ranking personnel are to be followed. Rejecting or not following these orders could result in action against the Service member, including negative career implications and even dishonorable discharge. Some of these orders could be to benefit the whole of society.

Similarly, as a member of a Military Department, Service members lack full autonomy and are subject to a variety of policies and instructions aimed at preserving the fighting force. In the context of health care, one such example is a DoD policy on influenza vaccinations. It is DoD policy that "all Active Duty and Reserve personnel be immunized against influenza with vaccines approved for their intended use by the Food and Drug Administration [FDA] and according to the recommendations of the Centers for Disease Control and

Prevention (CDC) and the Advisory Committee on Immunization Practices (ACIP)."[76] The point here is that the unit benefits if all are immunized, and immunizations maintain the health of the force. In this example, no individual may value their personal preferences over that of their unit. Moreover, military personnel are sometimes asked to incur risks not asked of civilians. In addition, DoD can also request approval to administer a non-FDA approved (i.e., experimental) vaccine, particularly if it is believed that such vaccines provide a critical potential countermeasure to a possible and plausible biological attack.

For example, in 1990, during Operation DESERT SHIELD, DoD anticipated the use of biological and chemical weapons. However, the only prophylactic products available to protect Service members were investigational new drugs (IND). As such, through discussions with the FDA, DoD requested that the FDA waive informed consent and other requirements related to IND status drugs. This request was granted in the form of a joint Health and Human Services and FDA Interim Rule waiving IND requirements in "certain military exigencies."[77] The White House directed FDA to develop regulations for such contingencies. Subsequently, FDA amended 21 Code of Federal Regulations 50.23, allowing an exception to the requirements for informed consent in this instance.[78]

3.4. Department of Defense Policies and Related Guidance

Numerous DoD and Military Department policies and rules dictate how military values are to be operationalized generally and in specific settings and contexts. Military health care professionals must adhere to these requirements as well as additional mandates specific to health care and the health care environment. In addition, several DoD entities have published guidance in the form of manuals and practice guidelines. What follows is a brief overview of policies and guidance relevant to ethical and expected conduct for military health care professionals.

General DoD Policies

DoDD 5500.07 Standards of Conduct (2007)
This DoD Directive (DoDD) orders all DoD agencies to administer and maintain a comprehensive agency ethics program, ensure compliance with several ethics policies, such as DoD 5500.7-R, "Joint Ethics Regulation" (see

below), certain provisions of Title 5, Code of Federal Regulations (which apply to administrative matters relevant to federal employees), and Executive Order 12674, "Principles of Ethical Conduct for Government Officers and Employees," which applies to all federal employees. The DoDD also requires that all DoD components ensure that all organizations within their jurisdiction administer and maintain a comprehensive ethics program. It exhorts all DoD personnel to perform their official duties lawfully and comply with the highest ethical standards, but does not describe those standards.[79]

DoD 5500.7-R, Joint Ethics Regulation (1993)

This Regulation provides a single source of standards of ethical conduct and ethics guidance, including direction in the areas of financial and employment disclosure systems, post-employment rules, enforcement, and training. It sets standards by which one should act based on values.[67]

> Values are core beliefs such as duty, honor, and integrity that motivate attitudes and actions. Not all values are ethical values (integrity is; happiness is not). Ethical values relate to what is right and wrong and thus take precedence over non-ethical values when making ethical decisions. DoD employees should carefully consider ethical values when making decisions as part of official duties.[67(p. 118)]

The values listed include honesty, integrity, loyalty, accountability, fairness, caring, respect, promise keeping, responsible citizenship, and pursuit of excellence. An ethical decision making plan is provided (see Figure 4).[3]

Define the Problem
Identify the Goal(s)
List Applicable Laws or Regulations
List the Ethical Values at Stake
Name All the Stakeholders
Gather Additional Information
State All Feasible Solutions
Eliminate Unethical Options
Rank Remaining Solutions
Commit To and Implement the Best Ethical Solution

From U.S. Department of Defense, 1993.[67]

Figure 4. DoD 550.7-R, Joint Ethics Regulation Ethical Decision-Making Plan.

DoDI 1300.21, Code of Conduct Training and Education (2001)

The Code of Conduct (CoC) addresses those situations and decision areas that, to some degree, all personnel could encounter, including basic information useful to U.S. prisoners of war (POWs) in efforts to survive honorably while resisting a captor's efforts to exploit them to the advantage of the enemy's cause and their own disadvantage. Such survival and resistance requires varying degrees of knowledge of the meaning of the six Articles of the CoC.[80]

Article I of the CoC applies to all Service members at all times. A member of the Armed Forces has a duty to support U.S. interests and oppose U.S. enemies regardless of the circumstances, whether located in a combat environment or in captivity. Medical personnel and chaplains are obligated to abide by the provisions of the CoC; however, their special retained status under the Geneva Conventions grants them some flexibility in its implementation and contains special exceptions should they be captured. Medical personnel, depending on their mission profile and employment capabilities, require varying levels of CoC training.[80]

DoD Policy and Related Guidance Specific to Health Care Professionals

DoD field manuals, guides, instructions, and Joint Publications provide guidance and instructions specific to health care professionals in a variety of settings and contexts, including stabilization or humanitarian missions and detainee installations. What follows is a sampling of relevant material from these documents. Highlighted are policies that discuss aspects of triage, the need to protect confidentiality, and issues related to cultural or host nation differences in resources and approaches to care.

FM 4-02.4 Medical Platoon Leaders' Handbook (Army) (2003)

This Army handbook assigns duties to the forward support medical company (FSMC) including treatment of patients with disease and nonbattle injuries, triage of mass casualties, advanced trauma management, initial resuscitation and stabilization, and evacuation of patients incapable of returning to duty from battalion aid stations to the FSMC. The Tables of Organization and Equipment (TOE) provide a model for fielding a unit at full capability, or at a reduced capability if resource constraints so mandate. The TOE also specifies the capabilities that the unit has to accomplish its mission. It also outlines the roles and responsibilities of the division surgeon (a Medical Corps officer), including ensuring the training and certification of division health care professionals, accurate recordkeeping and reporting, and briefing the division commander on all aspects and assets of health care operations in the division. Responsibilities are delineated for other medical personnel, such as the brigade surgeon and medical platoons. Detailed directions are outlined for anticipating large numbers of casualties, and augmentation of the medical platoon with one or more treatment teams. Chains of command and reporting are clearly outlined as are requirements for training and rehearsals.[81]

At a more detailed level, similarly the **Division and Brigade Surgeons' Handbook (Army)** (2000) outlines responsibilities regarding triage and evacuation. This guidance is procedural.[82]

DoD/Army Medical Department (AMEDD) Emergency War Surgery (2013)

This manual provides extensive guidance and instruction on handling mass casualties at multiple levels of care and evacuation. It notes that:

> Asymmetric warfare may further complicate the mass casualty event by inclusion of combatant, noncombatant, or third country nationals among the injured. The mass casualty demands a rapid transition from routine to contingency medical operations triggered by the earliest recognition of this specter within the fog of war. The transition will be eased by a mass casualty response plan that must be designed, exercised, and assessed to reflect relevant site and evacuation capability.[83(p.29)]

With regard to triage, it states:

> The ultimate goals of combat medicine are the return of the greatest possible number of warfighters to combat and the preservation of life, limb, and eyesight. The decision to withhold care from a casualty who in another less overwhelming situation might be salvaged is difficult for any physician, nurse, or medic. Decisions of this nature are unusual, even in mass casualty situations. Nonetheless, the overarching goal of providing the greatest good to the greatest number must guide these difficult decisions. Commitment of resources should be decided first based on the mission and immediate tactical situation and then by medical necessity, irrespective of a casualty's national or combatant status.[83(p.30)]

Prehospital Trauma Life Support, Eighth Edition (Military Version)

The tactical field care (TFC) chapter of this manual addresses the fact that military medics may be required to provide initial care for enemy combatants.

"Medically speaking, the tenets of trauma care do not change. Tactical considerations, however, add an extra dimension to the care of these casualties."[84]

The manual states that wounded, enemy personnel may still act as hostile combatants, employing any weapons or ordnance they are carrying:

> In Tactical Field Care, combat medical personnel should not attempt to provide medical care until the tactical situation permits and wounded hostile combatants have been rendered safe by other members of the unit. Rendering hostiles safe includes restraining them with flex cuffs or other devices, searching them for hidden weapons and ordnance, and segregating them from other captured hostiles. Once the medic is sure wounded hostile combatants have been rendered safe, medical care should be provided in accordance with TFC guidelines for US forces. Thereafter, the wounded hostiles should be safeguarded from further injury and sped to the rear as medically and tactically feasible.[84(p.172)]

Joint Publication 4-02 Health Service Support (2012)

This publication covers health care support provided in stabilization or humanitarian missions. It recommends approaches to dealing with supplies and standards in a host nation that do not meet U.S. standards of care or U.S.-approved sources. It addresses the need for plans regarding appropriate intervention procedures for prisoners on hunger strikes or who refuse treatment. It also notes the need to recognize cultural differences and ensure that adequate interpreters or translators and area specialists are appropriately planned to support medical operations. "Medical personnel should remain mindful of the fact that each force has a unique cultural identity."[85(p.VI-9)]

Joint Publication 3-07 Stability Operations (2011)

During stability operations the military may need to provide public health services for humanitarian reasons as well as to build community trust in the host nation government. Like Joint Publication 4-02, this publication provides doctrine for the conduct of stability operations during joint operations within the broader context of U.S. Government efforts.[85] It emphasizes that primary consideration must be given to supporting and supplementing existing medical infrastructure. The commander is instructed to "avoid operations that supplant existing public health and medical infrastructure or subvert longer-term plans."[85(p. III-26)]

The Joint Force Commander and Joint Staff Surgeon, in consultation with legal authorities, must "develop written guidance for the treatment and disposition of non-emergent and non-military patients that are consistent across the theater." 85(p. III-26) It cautions that although improving the host nation's public health systems fosters self-sufficiency and could result in accomplishing the U.S. military mission sooner, care must be taken to ensure that health care standards are appropriate for the local population and at a level that can be maintained by the existing host nation medical infrastructure.

Joint Publication 3-29 Foreign Humanitarian Assistance (2014)

According to Joint Publication 3-29, foreign humanitarian assistance (FHA) consists of:

> "DOD activities conducted outside the United States and its territories to directly relieve or reduce human suffering, disease, hunger, or privation. FHA includes foreign disaster relief (FDR) operations and other activities that directly address a humanitarian need, and may also be conducted concurrently with other DOD support missions and activities such as dislocated civilian support, security operations, and foreign consequence management (FCM). FHA operations (including FDR operations) are normally conducted in support of the United States Agency for International Development (USAID) or the Department of State (DOS).[86(p. I-1)]

Medical forces typically have three missions in FHA operations: force health protection, care for disaster victims, and assisting in reestablishing indigenous public health resources and institutions affected by the disaster. Medical planning should be integrated into overall response early and prior to deployment. "FHA operations may place US forces in situations that may substantially increase the risk of disease; food, water, blood products, high levels of industrial pollution, stress, fatigue, and indigenous diseases combine to provide a high-risk environment for all assigned personnel. This requires that the JTF [joint task force] have robust preventive medicine assets to perform medical and environmental health risk assessments and identify effective preventive medicine measures to counter the threat to US forces."[86(p. IV-23)]

Specific to humanitarian missions, medical forces might be asked to support local military and civilian health systems and provide direct public health care. If authorized, U.S. forces may also provide health care to foreign civilian populations on an urgent or emergent basis (within resource limitations) and return them to their national health systems at the earliest opportunity or when services can be provided by other agencies and organizations. Additionally, medical personnel may be called on to assist in reestablishing and supporting indigenous medical infrastructure, optimizing existent health systems, or identifying future foreign medical infrastructure improvements. U.S. military medical personnel do not routinely care for dislocated civilians unless specifically authorized.[86]

An extensive Appendix details considerations pre-, during, and post-deployment, concerning planning and execution, including the need to do an environmental assessment, and work with host nations and non-governmental organizations. Among the considerations is cultural competency:

> Cultural Aptitude. Health professionals with foreign language, cultural competency, and interagency experience are valuable in an FHA operation (i.e., US Air Force international health specialists [IHSs]) and Army special operations medical personnel).[86(p. E-3)]

Additional guidance on humanitarian assistance operations involving civilian and military operations are provided through United Nations Humanitarian Civil-Military Coordination frameworks,[87] as well as those of the International Red Cross.

DoDI 6495.02 Sexual Assault Prevention and Response Program Procedures (2013)

This Instruction requires that health care professionals maintain the confidentiality of a sexual assault victim unless an exception to restricted reporting applies. Health care personnel who make an unauthorized disclosure of a confidential communication are subject to disciplinary action pursuant to the Uniform Code of Military Justice or State statute, loss of privileges, or other adverse personnel or administrative actions.[88]

Policies Related to Disclosure of Protected Health Information

DoD faces a labyrinth of policies pertaining to what can and cannot be disclosed by a health care professional pertaining to private health information. DoDI 6025.18 (2009), "Privacy of Individually Identifiable Health Information in DoD Health Care Programs," states, "Health care entities shall, as authorized by and consistent with the procedures of Reference (c), ensure the availability to appropriate command authorities of health information concerning military personnel necessary to ensure the proper execution of the military mission."[89] Reference (c) is the Health Insurance Portability and Accountability Act (HIPAA) Privacy Rule, which "establishes national standards to protect individuals' medical records and other personal health information and applies to health plans, health care clearinghouses, and those health care providers that conduct certain health care transactions electronically. The Rule requires appropriate safeguards to protect the privacy of personal health information, and sets limits and conditions on the uses and disclosures that may be made of such information without patient authorization."[90]

However, DoD 6025.18-R, "DoD Health Information Privacy Regulation," (2003) lays out a series of circumstances in which protected health information may be used or disclosed, to include, for example:

- To determine the member's fitness for duty.
- To determine the member's fitness to perform any particular mission, assignment, order, or duty, including compliance with any actions required as a precondition to performance of such mission, assignment, order, or duty.
- To carry out any other activity necessary to the proper execution of the mission of the Armed Forces.[91]

DoDI 6490.04, "Mental Health Evaluations of Members of the Military Services (2013)," focuses on several aspects of evaluating Service members for mental health fitness and suitability for service. Military health care professionals qualified to conduct such evaluations must report results to commanders or supervisors, but in doing so "will make the minimum necessary disclosure and, when applicable, will advise how the commander or supervisor can assist the Service member's treatment."[92]

DoDI 6490.08, "Command Notification Requirements to Dispel Stigma in Providing Mental Health Care to Service Members (2011)," provides guidance for health care professionals for achieving balance between patient confidentiality rights and the command's right to know for operation and risk management decisions. Thus, it provides specific instructions for circumstances in which health care professionals might be obligated to violate a patient's confidentiality.[93]

Health care professionals are to presume that they are not to notify a Service member's commander when the Service member obtains mental health care or substance abuse education services, except under extenuating circumstances, such as the Service member presents a harm to himself or herself, to others, or to the mission. However, in such cases, the health care professional is to provide the minimal information necessary as required to satisfy the purpose of the disclosure.[93]

(See **Section 4** for further discussion of these issues, findings, and recommendations.)

Policies Related to Detainees and Internees

DoDI 2310.08E Medical Program Support for Detainee Operations (2006)

This Instruction "reaffirms the responsibility of health care personnel to protect and treat, in the context of a professional treatment relationship and established principles of medical practice, all detainees in the control of the Armed Forces during military operations. This includes enemy prisoners of war, retained personnel, civilian internees, and other detainees."[94(pi)] It further states that health care personnel have a "duty in all matters affecting the physical and mental health of detainees to perform, encourage, and support, directly and indirectly, actions to uphold the humane treatment of detainees and to ensure that no individual in the custody or under the physical control of the Department of Defense, regardless of nationality or physical location, shall be subject to cruel, inhuman, or degrading treatment or punishment, in accordance with and as defined in U.S. law."[94(p.2)]

It addresses the need to refuse to participate in punishment or procedures for applying physical restraints "unless such a procedure is determined to be necessary for the protection of the physical or mental health or the safety of the detainee, or necessary for the protection of other detainees or those treating, guarding, or otherwise interacting with them. Such restraints, if used, shall be applied in a safe and professional manner."[94(p.3)] It directs personnel to create and maintain accurate medical records, collecting only information that is related to the health care of the detainee, and to protect the privacy of the detainee. Such records have to be provided to the International Committee of the Red Cross when it is visiting detention facilities.

At 4.4.1, the Instruction states, "When the medical unit commander (or other designated senior medical activity officer) suspects the medical information to be disclosed may be misused, or if there is a disagreement between such medical activity officer and a senior officer requesting disclosure, the medical activity officer shall seek a senior command determination on the propriety of the disclosure or actions to ensure the use of the information will be consistent with applicable standards."[94(p.3-4)] If a health care professional observes or suspects a violation of these standards, he or she is to report the incident to the chain of command, and if not satisfied with the response to the Joint Staff Surgeon or relevant Surgeon General. "Other reporting mechanisms, such as the Inspector General, criminal investigation organizations, or Judge Advocates, also may be used."[94(p.4)]

Additional provisions relate to training requirements, the need to obtain consent for medical treatment or interventions with detainees. In addition, it states, "In the case of a hunger strike, attempted suicide, or other attempted serious self-harm, medical treatment or intervention may be directed without the consent of the detainee to prevent death or serious harm. Such action must be based on a medical determination that immediate treatment or intervention is necessary to prevent death or serious harm, and, in addition, must be approved by the commanding officer of the detention facility or other designated senior officer responsible for detainee operations."[94(p.5)]

Medical Treatment of Hunger Strikers (DoDI 2310.08E, 2006)

DoDI 2310.08E states that health care professionals are to "uphold the humane treatment of detainees and to ensure that no individual in the custody or under the physical control of the Department of Defense...shall be subject to cruel, inhuman, or degrading treatment or punishment..."[94(p.2)] Health care professionals caring for detainees also "have a duty to protect detainees' physical and mental health and provide appropriate treatment of disease."[94(p.2)]

Paragraph 4.7 says "[i]n general, health care will be provided with the consent of the detainee. To the extent practicable, standards and procedures for obtaining consent will be consistent with those applicable to consent from other patients."[94(p.4)] It also states "In the case of a hunger strike, attempted suicide, or other attempted self-harm, medical treatment or intervention may be directed without the consent of the detainee to prevent death or serious harm. Such action must be based on a medical determination that immediate treatment or intervention is necessary to prevent death or serious harm, and, in addition, must be approved by the commanding officer of the detention facility or other designated senior officer responsible for detainee operations."[94(p.5)] A 2009 review panel found that DoD policy for treatment of hunger strikers is similar to that used by the U.S. Federal Bureau of Prisons, as authorized in Title 28, Code of Federal Regulations, Part 549.[95]

Related to this, a Joint Task Force Guantanamo Bay (JTF-GTMO), Cuba, Joint Medical Group, Standard Operating Procedures for Medical Management of Detainees (05 Mar 2013) provides detailed instructions and algorithms for medical management of hunger strikers including protocols for involuntary feeding, which requires a documented order from the JTF-GTMO Commander, followed by notification of the Commander U. S. Southern Command, the Joint Staff, and relevant DoD offices.[96] Specific criteria are provided for consideration by the Medical Officer in recommending involuntary treatment. This issue will be discussed further later in this document, under the Geneva Conventions.

Joint Publication 3-63 Detainee Operations (2008)

The relevant part of this publication relates to the responsibilities of the Medical Officer/Surgeon in detainee operations. Importantly, it states that the Medical Officer/Surgeon is to maintain a chain of command independent of the guard forces. Among the duties are:

- Coordinate actions of medically qualified personnel
- Provide first responder capability to the detainee population
- Coordinate forward resuscitative care or higher capability
- Advise the commander on medical and health-related issues
- Coordinate medical consultations with appropriate medical specialists and coordinates for transportation and escort of detainees to appointments, if required
- Coordinate with the civil affairs officer to ensure detainee medical concerns are being considered for possible presentation at the civil-military operations center
- Ensure the medical requirements within the detention facility are met consistent with Department of Defense Instruction 2310.08E, Medical Program Support for Detainee Operations, and its implementing orders and programs.[97]

DoD/AMEDD Emergency War Surgery (2013)

This publication also addresses medical care of internees. It states that, whenever possible, internees should receive medical care equal to that given to U.S. troops. It directs that health care professionals "have a responsibility to report information that constitutes a clear and imminent threat to the lives and welfare of others." Further:

> Providers should report any suspected abuse or maltreatment of an internee. Providers should inform the theater internment facility chain of

command of internee physical limitations. Medical recommendations concerning internee activities are nonbinding. Decisions concerning internee activities are made by the chain of command. Healthcare providers charged with the care of internees should not be actively involved in interrogation, advise interrogators how to conduct interrogations, or interpret individual medical records/medical data for the purposes of interrogation or intelligence gathering. Healthcare personnel ordered to perform duties they deem unethical should request to be recused through his or her chain of command. If the situation is not resolved satisfactorily, healthcare providers may contact their Command Surgeon or the Inspector General. Requirements for internee care are provided in AR 190-8/OPNAVINST 3461.6/AFJI 31-304/MCO 3461.1.[98(pp.462-463)]

Additional International Policy: The Geneva Conventions

The Geneva Conventions are a series of treaties on the treatment of civilians, POWs, and soldiers who are otherwise rendered "outside the fight" or incapable of fighting. The first Convention was drafted by the International Committee for Relief to the Wounded (which became the International Committee for the Red Cross and Red Crescent). This convention produced a treaty designed to protect wounded and sick soldiers during wartime. The Swiss Government agreed to hold the Conventions in Geneva, and a few years later, a similar agreement to protect shipwrecked soldiers was produced. In 1949 at the end of World War II, two new Conventions were added to the original two, and all four were ratified by a number of countries. The 1949 versions of the Conventions, along with two additional Protocols, are in force today. Of relevance here, Convention 1 protects wounded and infirm soldiers and medical personnel against attack, execution without judgment, torture, and assaults upon personal dignity. It also grants them the right to proper medical treatment and care. Medical personnel have to be exclusively assigned to medical duties in order to enjoy the specific protection to which they are entitled. If the medical assignment is permanent, respect and protection are due at all times. Protocol I requires that "if needed, all available help shall be afforded to civilian medical personnel in an area where civilian medical services are disrupted by reason of combat activity."[99] Protocol II requires that medical personnel "be granted all available help for the performance of their duties."[100]

With regard to triage, the Geneva Conventions state:

> The only reason that can justify priority in the order of treatment are reasons of medical urgency. This is not so much an exception to the principle of equality of treatment of the wounded as it is recognition of the legitimacy of triage. So long as adversary patients are triaged on an equal footing with allied patients, triage is justified. An adversary can never refuse to care for adversary wounded on the pretext that his adversary has abandoned them without medical personnel and equipment.[101]

3.5. Conclusion

Extensive guidance, instruction, and doctrine have been issued relevant to the expectations and responsibilities of health care professionals in a variety of military contexts. **Section 4** highlights some areas where guidance might be confusing and **Section 5** stresses the need for easy accessibility to policies and instructions through education and training and self-seeking resources.

4. ETHICAL ISSUES IN MILITARY MEDICAL SETTINGS

4.1. Introduction and Background on the Military Health System

Military health care professionals serve in a variety of settings, more diverse than is found in the civilian environment. The Military Health System (MHS) is a global, comprehensive, integrated system that includes combat medical services, peacetime health care delivery, public health services, medical education and training, and medical research and development. MHS personnel provide a continuum of health services from austere operational environments through remote, fixed military treatment facilities (MTFs) to major tertiary care medical centers distributed across the United States. The MHS combines health care resources to provide access to care for the 9.6 million beneficiaries, including Service members of the seven uniformed services, National Guard and Reserve members, retirees and their eligible family members, survivors, certain former spouses, and other individuals, while maintaining the capability to support military operations worldwide.

Force Health Protection is a critical support function of the MHS in providing a worldwide deployable defense force. As of May 2014, there were nearly 1.4 million current members of the Armed Forces. Since the onset of the conflicts in Afghanistan and Iraq, until the end of 2013, 2.6 million troops have been deployed, all of who had to be medically ready, and uniformed medical personnel have deployed in support of combat operations on a continuous basis.[64] Military health care professionals are also expected to care for detainees, enemy combatants, nonstate actors, local nationals, and coalition forces. In addition, U.S. military personnel are often deployed to assist in humanitarian missions, such as natural disasters or to provide care to local citizens in combat zones.

Sessums et al.[102] note that in the combat or austere environment, challenging ethical decisions often have to be made by relatively junior primary care physicians (battalion surgeons). These physicians and other health care professionals might be tasked with responsibilities for which they were not specifically trained, such as working with the civilian population to facilitate military operations. They might have only received a few weeks' notice of deployment, and if in the National Guard or Reserve Component, might be leaving behind a civilian job and responsibilities to patients, peers, and institutions at home. They are not likely to have trained with their unit or been the beneficiaries of advance training that involves extensive briefings or field exercises. Once deployed, they might work under dual chains of command, the line and the medical officer.

Thus, while military health care professionals face all of the same ethical dilemmas found in the civilian health care sector, they can face even more within the context of military medicine. This section focuses briefly on some unique ethical dilemmas that can arise in the context of military medicine. Much has already been written about these issues; the reader is encouraged to consult the Textbooks of Military Medicine series on *Military Medical Ethics*[1] for a complete perspective.

4.2. Fitness for Duty Examinations and Screening: Disclosure to the Command

Military health care professionals described challenges in responding to commanders who sometimes request more information on a patient's health status than may be appropriate or necessary. Patient concerns regarding release of information to leadership can alter the therapeutic relationship between providers and their patients and lead some Service members to withhold certain information or seek care in the civilian sector. In contrast, if a Service member discusses personal health concerns or psychological health problems with a chaplain, the chaplain has special privileges that protect him or her from being ordered or asked to breach the Service member's privacy.

For example, personnel reported concerns when working with individuals suffering with post-traumatic stress disorder, because if the condition is reported to the command it might affect the Service member's military career. With increased concerns regarding both suicide prevention and ensuring patients are not a danger to themselves, others, or the mission, significant pressure has been placed on some health care professionals to provide more information to more elements of leadership than may ordinarily seem appropriate. As described in **Section 3,** DoD doctrine requires that health care professionals, as covered entities under the Health Insurance Portability and Accountability Act (HIPAA) Privacy Rule, protect a patient's private health information. However, military necessity may blur the lines, as a review of several DoD Instructions in **Section 3** also highlighted.

Military health care professionals reported to the Subcommittee a lack of clarity in policies regarding the level of detail that should routinely be provided to commanders regarding a military member's health status and treatment. There also appears to be a mixed message in current guidance: comply with the HIPAA Privacy Rule for Service members, but release information to commanders if there is a potential impact on the mission. Without clear guidance, each provider has to determine whether there is potential for impact, and each might have a different threshold for disclosure.

The nature of the guidance regarding release of protected health information of Service members for military necessity creates the potential for tension between a health care professional's duty to the patient in terms of protecting their privacy, the military mission, and the commander's need for information to ensure successful execution of the mission, maintain readiness, and protect the unit.

It is also the duty of a health care professional to ensure the medical fitness of a Service member either prior to deployment or redeployment or in return to duty following an injury or illness. Less experienced providers might feel pressure from the command to return someone to active duty or to the battlefield against their professional judgment, for example, a Sailor who has experienced depression or a Soldier who has recently experienced an explosive blast. Health care professionals who met with the Subcommittee indicated that establishing and maintaining communication and trust with the line command is important to avoiding and resolving issues of this nature. Advance training on ethical and policy obligations could also help clarify the responsibilities of the health care professionals.

Finding 6

Military health care professionals report a lack of clarity in policies regarding the level of detail that should routinely be provided to commanders regarding a military member's health status and treatment. Without clear guidance, each provider has to determine whether there is potential for impact, and each provider might have a different threshold for disclosure.

Recommendation 6

DoD should develop clear guidance on what private health information can be communicated by health care professionals to leadership, and the justifications for exceptions to the rule for reasons of military necessity.

Finding 7

Lawyers and Chaplains are afforded unique status and privileges with respect to the confidential relationships they have with military personnel seeking their services.

Recommendation 7

DoD should provide military health care professionals with privileges similar to those of Chaplains and Judge Advocates regarding their independence and obligation to protect privacy and confidentiality while meeting the requirements of line commanders.

4.3. Treatment Priorities or Triage for Casualties in the Military Setting

The battlefield is a particularly challenging setting in which to provide health care. "It is violent. It is noisy. It is chaotic. It is in constant flux. And it is unpredictable."[1(p.371)] In addition, resources might be limited and the uncertainty of resupply can force difficult decisions. Demands on resources can create conflict. For example, line commanders might request the use of medical evacuation assets to remove troops killed in action from the battlefield, which can lead to conflicts over use of limited resources.[1(p.372)] Fatigue and constant stress can impede clear thinking. Health care professionals might not have the time to consider and weigh all options. One of the most difficult ethical situations in the heat of battle can be in setting treatment priorities and triage for casualties.

In the health care setting, triage typically refers to the principled process used by health care professionals to prioritize the care of certain patients over others in a way that responsibly allocates resources. For example, in the emergency department, a patient with a broken finger would be likely to wait to see a radiologist behind a patient brought in from a traumatic car accident. The principle is to first attend to the care of patients in most need of medical attention. Decisions are likely to be made based on the availability of nurses or physician specialists, the number of beds available, or the availability of medical supplies and medicines.

In the battlefield, where there might be mass casualties of a similar nature, and where resources might be limited, there are generally three categories considered for triage: 1) patients who will live without medical care and only require minor treatment interventions, 2) those who will die if they do not receive medical care, and 3) those who will die regardless of whether they receive care.[103-105] Beam further parses the battlefield environment into three categories: non-austere, austere, and extreme.[106]

In the battlefield environment, line commanders might ask health care professionals to alter the triage conditions and treat the least injured first so that they can return to duty and protect the unit. This request would be consistent with the commander's fiduciary obligation to win the battle at the least cost to his unit.[103] Beam emphasizes that such realignment of triage would only be justified in the extreme environment—that is, to preserve the strength of the fighting force—and should be extremely rare.[106]

Adams suggests that a number of conditions must be met before a commander considers the environment so extreme that reverse triage procedures should be used, for example, the chance that returning the mildly wounded to battle will make a significant difference in winning the present battle. Adams also notes that the extreme conditions triage model is rarely used.[103] It is also important to add that the extreme triage conditions are not aligned with the Geneva Conventions, which state, "Only urgent medical reasons will authorize priority in the order of treatment to be administered."[107]

Return to duty can also be an important consideration in the austere environment, where health care professionals can face similar conflicts about how to save as many lives as possible while preserving the strength of the fighting force.

The 1994 edition of the Army Field Manual (FM 8-55) shifted the emphasis away from a previous focus on returning soldiers to duty as soon as possible. It provides the following order of priorities when priorities are in conflict:

1) Maintain medical presence with the soldier.
2) Maintain the health of the command.
3) Save lives.
4) Clear the battlefield.
5) Provide state-of-the-art care.
6) Return soldiers to duty as early as possible.[108]

Recent guidance from Tactical Combat Casualty Care specifies the importance of adhering to triage procedures in all cases except management of wounded hostile combatants. As described in **Section 3,** no care can be provided until the combatant indicates surrender, drops all weapons, and is proven to no longer pose a threat.[84(p.712)]

The goal here is not to prescribe what the triage and treatment priority policies and practices should be in a given setting. Rather, it is to emphasize that the complexity of the conditions under which triage and treatment priorities must be decided warrant ample advance training and exposure to the possible scenarios that a health care professional could confront in the austere or extreme environment. In addition, Sessums et al emphasize "They need to know the law applicable to deployed physicians as well as the treatment algorithms for the resuscitation of trauma patients they are likely to treat."[102(p.445)] They also need to know the law in the jurisdiction in which they are licensed. The complexity and possibility for resulting moral injury on the part of the health care professional tasked with making difficult choices also suggest that some sort of debriefing process, either during or after deployment, be in place to help individuals work through and justify difficult ethical decisions made under duress.

4.4. Humanitarian Assistance, Disaster Response, and Medical Support Missions

The U.S. military has a long tradition of providing humanitarian relief after war or natural disaster.[109] In recent years, the U.S. military is increasingly providing medical support for U.S. forces, coalition forces, and civilian populations in a broad range of missions including peace operations, humanitarian assistance, disaster relief, and nation assistance. Most recently, U.S. personnel have deployed to assist West Africa to assist in the Ebola outbreak.[110] Typically, such endeavors are guided by a mission statement, which outlines the roles and responsibilities of participating organizations. DoD doctrine guides medical planning for such operations (see **Section 4**). Often U.S. personnel are working with or coordinating the efforts of non-U.S. military personnel, other U.S. federal agencies, or non-governmental organizations. Sometimes these missions occur in concert with supporting the deploying force. It is important to plan engagements of this nature to avoid unintended consequences of seemingly positive and helpful actions which may in the long term undermine host nation institutions or create expectations for support that cannot be sustained.

In other circumstances, U.S. personnel are mentoring host nation health care providers; that is, not actually providing care, but serving as medical advisors. The Subcommittee was briefed on the challenges military medical mentors assigned to a host nation hospital had working in an environment where host nation corruption, mismanagement, and lack of accountability resulted in continual neglect and maltreatment of patients.[111]

These missions can raise unique and different challenges for health care professionals than those found in military operations, for example, wide variations in medical assets and practices among coalition members and variability in medical readiness among coalition forces. The medical assets of coalition partners may be inadequate for the mission, or misused or misallocated.[111-113] Differences in standards of care and medical practice from country to country can pose ethical dilemmas for health care professionals. For example, some militaries may have lower standards of care than the United States with regard to treating traumatic injury and infection. U.S. personnel can be challenged to maintain quality control in a clinic setting staffed with medical personnel of forces from developing nations.

In operations involving disaster relief, humanitarian assistance, or refugee populations, the medical mission may reach well beyond supporting the deploying force. There might be pressing needs of the civilian population, including those of women and children. There might be cultural differences in how women and children should be treated, in what order of priority, and by whom. The August 2014 guidance for the Expeditionary Medical Support and Air Force Theater Hospital describes standard of care for Humanitarian Assistance and Disaster Relief operations as follows:

Medics should apply U.S. medical standards when treating American forces. The medical [rules of engagement] define the scope of care and triage guidelines for host nation patients based on the situation, other available health support capabilities, patient movement capabilities, and the host nation's request for support. Medical interventions typically are limited to procedures and therapies that are low risk, can be performed quickly, require limited follow-up, and do not undermine the host nation medical system.[114]

As described in **Section 3**, health care professionals have an obligation to help with urgent medical problems and will have an understandable desire to respond to medical need, regardless of the official mission.

Finding 8
Cultural norms, social expectations, and rules of engagement can create unique challenges for those providing care to non-U.S. personnel or serving as medical mentors to developing world host nation personnel. Providing care in the context of humanitarian assistance or disaster relief operations may involve unique stressors in coping with extensive unmet health care needs with limited resources. Health care professionals would benefit from having a thorough understanding of the issues associated with these operations including the underlying cultural beliefs, social expectations, resource limitations, and altered treatment priorities associated with these environments.

Recommendation 8
DoD should provide specific education and training for health care professionals designated to serve as medical mentors or health care providers in foreign health care facilities or in support of humanitarian assistance or disaster relief operations. Such training should cover cultural differences, potential ethical issues, rules of engagement, and actions that might be taken to avert, report, and address unethical, criminal, or negligent behavior or practices.

4.5. Detainee Installations

Detainee installations can provide unique challenges for health care professionals who are required to provide routine health care to detainees, assess the ability of detainees to undergo lawful forms of interrogation, accurately report health status in medical records, and respond to hunger strikes, some of which can be prolonged. Highly publicized abuses of prisoners at Abu Ghraib shined a light on the role and complicity of military medical personnel in physical or psychological abuse of prisoners. Force feeding of detainees at Guantanamo Bay raised questions about the role of medical personnel in providing involuntary treatment and their professional rights on moral and legal grounds to refuse participating in such procedures.[3,4,102,115] Numerous investigations at the departmental and congressional levels have revealed lapses of health care providers in accurately documenting and reporting abuses.[95,116-118] These events have moved professional groups to reassert their positions and for DoD and the Military Departments to review their policies and procedures.

As described in **Section 2,** the ethical codes of health care professional groups universally condemn the involvement of their members in any form of physical or psychological abuse. As described in **Section 3,** evolving DoD policy and guidance has clarified the responsibilities of health care professionals in such settings.

4.6. Deployments and Professional Support

Like any Service member, military health care professionals face uncertainty throughout their careers in terms of postings, relocations, and deployments. National Guard and Reserve Component personnel face the prospect of last minute assignments and deployments that take them away from their civilian employment and community. Deployments to combat zones can be intense and stressful. The ways in which medical officers train and deploy can exacerbate the potential for future issues. Insufficient opportunity to debrief after returning from deployment may also be a missed opportunity to prevent or mitigate moral injury in some individuals or groups. (see **Section 2**).

Fostering a Culture of Support
Health care professionals cannot always resolve ethical conflicts alone. Resources and support are needed for addressing conflicts and raising an issue up the medical chain of command. The military values integrity, and support of an individual's ethics is consistent with that value. Most military health care professionals understand that mission requirements may limit their autonomy in patient care decisions. If appropriate communication and training occurs

(see **Section** 5), the likelihood of conflict or the desire to recuse oneself from certain actions may be less likely to occur. However, when it does, institutional support, policies, and a culture must be in place to allow individuals with legitimate concerns to express and act on them. When institutional ethics go awry, individuals must feel empowered as moral agents to report problems and challenge the institution. They must have ready access to policies and instructions that can guide their decision making. Because military health care professionals have diminished autonomy compared to their civilian counterparts, special actions must be taken to protect and support the ethical autonomy that does exist. In addition, the Subcommittee heard from medical officers that line commanders are not always fully aware of the special codes of conduct and ethical principles to which health care professionals must adhere.

Finding 9

DoD does not have an online portal to provide efficient access to medical ethics information and resources.

Recommendation 9

DoD should create an online medical ethics portal. At a minimum, it should include links to relevant policies, guidance, laws, education, training, professional codes, and military consultants in medical ethics.

Finding 10

It is not evident that line leadership always has a clear understanding of the roles, responsibilities, and limitations of health care professionals with respect to what actions they may or may not take and what information they may or may not provide based on ethical codes, licensure standards of conduct, and legal restrictions.

Recommendation 10

DoD should include in professional military education courses information on the legal and ethical limitations on health care professionals regarding patient care actions they may or may not take in supporting military operations and patient information they may and may not communicate to line leadership.

Post-Deployment Issues

Anecdotally, in meeting with Subcommittee members, some active duty Service members described difficulties with deploying as individuals, without the opportunity to train or bond with their unit prior to deployment. This is discussed further in Section 5.

U.S. military health care professionals who had deployed indicated to the Subcommittee that having an opportunity to debrief and decompress, particularly following deployments that involved intensely emotional experiences, may be of benefit in coping with any moral injury and reducing the sense of isolation. It also provides an opportunity to identify those who need additional help. Some health care professionals reported that due to short staffing at their MTFs, they were immediately put back on the clinic or operating room schedule with little or no time off following deployment and little recognition of what they may have experienced. The opportunity to debrief and decompress following deployment is consistent with current doctrine, [119,120] although effectiveness may depend on the methods and target population.[121]

The Subcommittee was briefed on the British system, in which post-deployment actions include a brief stopover for personnel to decompress from any intense experiences they encountered during deployment, a mandatory return to their training establishment to complete post-deployment processing including an assessment of their well-being, and an additional opportunity for key personnel to pass on lessons learned during training events for those preparing to deploy.

In addition, military health care professionals usually deploy from active positions at MTFs. As such, other members of the medical team must compensate for the individual who has left on a deployment, taking on additional patients and responsibilities. This situation can lead to additional stress when the Service member is expected to return directly to work upon their return, where there might be little empathy or support for what the individual might have encountered while deployed. These demands of the MTF could prevent the Service member from properly debriefing and reintegrating back into life in garrison while coming to terms with any challenging situations experienced while deployed.

Members of the National Guard and Reserve expressed to the Subcommittee different concerns than those on active duty, potentially due to the inherent differences between these two positions. Individuals did not express the same level of difficulty in deploying as individuals, with one Service member noting that when they are comfortable with their military and medical role, they can easily integrate into a new unit. While levels of ethical training also varied significantly, they did not express the same level of concern in joining other units. However, the National Guard and Reserve members did describe similar difficulties upon returning from deployment. They noted that because they are situated in civilian communities, they lack some of the military infrastructure and support systems available to active duty members. They also noted the difficulty in leaving civilian careers for deployments, citing that civilian employers often grow less supportive as multiple deployments take away from time at civilian health care centers.

Finding 11

Military health care professionals could benefit from opportunities for debriefing, particularly following deployments that involved intensely emotional experiences, as a means of coping with moral injury and reducing their sense of isolation. Debriefing may also provide an opportunity to identify those who need additional help post-deployment.

Recommendation 11

DoD should ensure that systems and processes are in place for debriefing health care professionals to help them transition home following deployment. Debriefing should occur as a team when possible. Not only could this help mitigate potential moral injury in health care professionals, but it may also provide lessons learned and case studies for inclusion in ongoing training programs.

Finding 12

Having senior medical officers as full members of the Commander's staff provides an opportunity for regular two-way communication. Medical leaders would have insight to key goals, issues, and concerns of the command while also ensuring that the Commander is aware of medical limitations and potential ethical concerns in planning and operations.

Recommendation 12

To create an environment that promotes ethical conduct and minimizes conflicts of dual loyalty, DoD leadership should emphasize that senior military health care professionals are full members of the Commander's staff as an advisor on medical ethics as it relates to military readiness.

5. ETHICS EDUCATION AND TRAINING

5.1. Introduction

Military health care professionals receive ethics guidance in the form of both formal education and military training. One noteworthy source of military specific ethics education for health care professionals is the Uniformed Services University of the Health Sciences (USUHS). However, most military health care professionals have not attended USUHS, joining the military after receiving education in the civilian sector. These individuals receive some level of traditional medical ethics instruction through their formal education and receive military ethics guidance through subsequent military training. The level, intensity, and nature of ethics education is likely to vary based on the specific civilian institution. However, outside of annual ethics training regarding behavior relevant to finances and relationships with contractors, ethics training has been described as limited and inconsistent across the Military Departments.

Educational programs that focus on ethical issues are by necessity complex and must accommodate the reality that ethical dilemmas are often not straightforward or clear cut and may involve quandaries about which well-informed persons of good will can reasonably disagree. Thus, well-designed ethics education programs will cover basic ethical principles as well as provide health care professionals with many perspectives on the issues they might confront. The goal should be to provide a framework to guide the reasoning processes one might use in drawing conclusions that are consistent with one's moral values but for which all others might not necessarily agree. Such programs should provide individuals with the tools and reasoning needed to justify actions, especially when under scrutiny and to facilitate open dialogue with others before, during, and after a moral dilemma. In the context of military medical ethics education, the goal should be to provide individuals with a basic understanding of the ethical principles that apply, the circumstances in which they might arise, and strategies for addressing them, if not resolving them.

5.2. fundamentals of Ethics Education and Training

In developing a model curriculum for ethics in public health, authors Jennings et al describe fundamental goals of ethics education. The authors elaborate on these goals:[122]

1) *Stimulating the Moral Imagination.* "Stimulating the moral imagination involves the ability to gain a feel for the lives of others, some sense of the motions and the feelings that are provoked by difficult ethical choices, and some insight into how moral viewpoints influence the way individuals live their lives. And the goal is not simply to stimulate but also to broaden the moral imagination—to begin with what people at first feel to be right or good, but then to deepen and sometimes to challenge and change those feelings by transforming them into more reflective judgments and more sophisticated and well-informed convictions."(p. 5)
2) *Recognizing Ethical Issues.* "Ethics education is not unlike scientific education in one respect: it involves a certain structuring of perception, a certain kind of "seeing as." To see a certain state of affairs or decision as a moral issue is to see that it raises considerations of human value, and that it has significant implications for harms or benefits human beings experience."(p.5)
3) *Developing Analytical Skills.* "Ethical analysis involves the use of a certain set of prescriptive and evaluative categories, such as rights, duties, virtue, justice, responsibility, freedom, respect, dignity, and well-being. Participants need to acquire the ability to use these concepts in constructing arguments that are logical, consistent, and defensible in the face of reasoned disagreement and challenge."(p.5)
4) *Eliciting a Sense of Moral Obligation and Responsibility.* "Ethics discussions usually start with simple assumptions and beliefs, challenge them, and replace them with more nuanced thinking. In this way, ethical analysis sometimes makes moral choice more, not less, difficult and complex."(p. 5-6)
5) *Coping with Moral Ambiguity.* "It is simply a fact of life that we must learn to tolerate disagreements and to accept the inevitable ambiguities that arise when examining ethical problems. Many ethical issues admit of no final, clear resolution." (p. 6)

Stephen Behnke, Director of the Ethics Office, the American Psychological Association, outlined four points regarding ethics training: 1) consider the legal, clinical, ethical, and risk management contexts in assessing ethical questions (the "four-bin" approach), employing a process of differentiation and integration, in which a question is analyzed in relation to other questions and issues associated with the specific situation; 2) assess where there is clarity and where there is ambiguity or uncertainty, in which professional judgment and discretion are exercised; 3) recognize that ethical decision making involves the application of skills, not simply memorization of rules or principles; and 4) determine how to integrate ethics and human rights in a helpful way.[123,124]

A number of publications have included tools to assist decision making in the context of assessing dual loyalty issues. Williams provides an analysis of the term "dual loyalty," providing examples from both civilian and military health care scenarios, and summarizes a process for ethical decision making in this context.

In the last chapter of the second volume of the textbook of *Military Medical Ethics*, Beam and Howe propose a military medical ethic and provide a decision matrix to assist in military medical ethics decision making, along with an algorithm to assist with decision making when there are conflicts between ethics and the law.[125]

Physicians for Human Rights and the University of Cape Town published a report titled "Dual Loyalty & Human Rights in Health Professional Practice; Proposed Guidelines & Institutional Mechanisms"[44] with detailed guidance to assist in ethical decision making, including a section devoted to military health professionals. They also suggest that improving institutional structures and training would contribute significantly to enhancing ethical practice in health care when dual loyalty issues arise.

The 2008 IOM workshop on Military Medical Ethics: Issues Regarding Dual Loyalties provided illustrative discussions and examples on this topic. It also included an example of a tool adapted for assessing the human rights impact of public health policies and interventions to assist ethical decision making during disaster response and humanitarian assistance missions.[2]

Ethics education and training programs take a variety of pedagogical approaches. Currently, nearly half of American medical schools mandate an introductory course in ethics as part of their core curriculum. A 2004 survey of medical schools found that most offer some formal instruction in medical ethics, and among these, many offer it in required preclinical courses.[126] A similar study of nursing indicates that about 50 percent of registered nurses receive formal ethics training in their professional training, and that about 20 percent reported no training at all.[127] At the nurse practitioner level, most programs require some formal ethics training, with 20 contact hours being the mean.[128] Many programs at the undergraduate and graduate level state that ethics education is integrated throughout the curriculum, making standardization and quantification difficult and instructor-dependent.[127]

There is significant variation in the content, method, and timing of ethics education for health professionals. In general, medical ethics programs integrate lectures and case studies. Students learn about current issues in medicine and may participate in mock ethical consultations or clinical rounds. Many academic institutions have some form of curricula in medical ethics. Curriculum design sometimes focuses on published studies of the ethical dilemmas seen in inpatient settings, outpatient settings, or consultation settings.

In addition to resources developed at academic institutions the World Health Organization developed "The modules of Medical Ethics for Medical Undergraduates" to help medical students "recognize the importance of being sensitive to ethical issues within everyday clinical practice and develop in them the ability to effectively address ethical concerns of patients as well as in clinical research involving patients and human beings."[129] The module covers 1) practice according to statutory requirements and codes of conduct for medical practice; 2) need to demonstrate sensitivity to ethical issues and ethical behavior in professional practice; 3) ethical principles in conducting research; and 4) approaches to analyzing ethical issues and makes ethical decisions in medical practice.

Despite the inclusion of ethics into American medical school curriculums and the availability of a variety of outside learning modules, it is important to emphasize the variation in amount, quality, and relevance of ethics education and training that may exist across health care professions prior to entry into the military. Such differences highlight the need for additional ethical training and education upon entry into a Military Department. This subsequent education and training should promote a more uniform level of ethical expertise.

5.3. Current DoD Medical Ethics Education and Training Landscape

USUHS, as the nation's only federal health sciences university, maintains a core commitment to medical ethics. The Graduate Students' Code on the

Responsible Conduct of Science lays out basic responsibilities and principles, highlighting the core values of the university including honesty, integrity, respect and humane research behavior.[130] Each of the four program areas within the university includes at least one mandatory course in ethics. While course hours vary, the theme of ethics is also integrated into a variety of other courses. This integration also includes the Bushmaster field exercise, a four-day field exercise where "several operational problems directly challenge the student to recognize and address ethical conflicts in their role as a provider in [military] conflicts."[131]

Within the medical school, ethics are formally taught in the pre-clerkship phase of the curriculum, in the Medical Ethics course. Within the course, students are exposed to a variety of topics including the student/patient relationship, reproduction, genetics, withholding life sustaining treatment, translating ethics into practice, military medicine, and disabilities. The session on military medicine discusses the ethical, legal, and social aspects of medical care and includes small group discussion. This discussion is based on a number of scenarios such as addressing enemy combatants; withholding pain medications; disclosing medical information that may affect flight status; and reporting potential shortcomings of staffing in a military hospital.[131] Students are required to attend all sessions that involve advanced reading, panel presentations, and facilitated small groups. A session on military ethics involves a facilitated small group discussion that addresses 13 cases involving unique military scenarios frequently dealing with conflict between the military physician as both a physician and military officer.

Ethics is also woven through the new curriculum of the Molecules to Military Medicine program. Initiated with the class of 2015, the new curriculum is designed to "keep pace with the changing needs of the military and public health systems."[132] Changes to the previous program included "better integration of the basic and clinical sciences, earlier exposure to learning in the hospital setting and careful attention to assessing student competency throughout all four years."[132] During the pre-clerkship phase of this updated medical curriculum, students attend a Military Contingency Medicine course focused on the military physician's staff role to the commander, introducing a variety of scenarios where students must address conflict between their role as a physician and a staff officer. These themes are continued in military exercises including command briefings; planning missions requiring students to balance the medical and military demands with the constraints of their dual roles; stability operation laboratories where students balance the provision of medical care to the host nation with the mission of the U.S. military; and exercises where students must create and prepare comprehensive analyses and recommendations to their commander.[131] The curriculum involves didactic, experiential, and field exercises. While USUHS medical school graduates make up only about 10 percent of annual accessions of new physicians into the military, it is estimated that 25 percent of active duty physicians and approximately one-third of physicians in medical leadership positions are USUHS graduates.[133]

Students within the school of nursing are also required to take courses in ethics. Ethics and Policy in Federal Health Systems is a required course for all Doctor of Nursing Practice students. This course provides students with frameworks to guide ethical decision making, examining the various factors involved in health care delivery and policy. Another core course from this program is Population Health and Epidemiology in Advanced Practice, where ethical population health concepts are introduced including health disparities and social justice. Additionally, the Translating Evidence into Practice course includes a module dedicated to addressing ethical implications of translating new scientific discoveries into practice. Ethics courses are also included within the Doctorate of Philosophy Nursing Program, such as Ethics in Science and Research Ethics.[134]

Within the Department of Preventive Medicine and Biometrics, some graduate degrees require a course on "Ethics in Public Health" and "Ethics and the Responsible Conduct of Research." Ethics topics are also woven into a number of other courses offered.[135]

Ethics are addressed throughout the graduate dental curriculum. As specified by the Commission on Dental Education, the dental program ensures that students/residents "are able to demonstrate the application of the principles of ethical reasoning, ethical decision making and professional responsibility as they pertain to the academic environment, research, patient care, and practice management."[136] In addition to a medical and legal seminar during orientation on research ethics, during their senior year students receive a seminar on medical and general ethical issues from the past Department Chair of Philosophy at the U.S. Air Force Academy. The Federal Services Dental Educators annual workshop also includes ethics as a curriculum topic.

Within the psychology department, students are required to complete a course on ethics and the conduct of responsible research prior to advancing to candidacy. The course "Ethics and the Responsible Conduct of Research" reviews basic principles for responsible research including ethical responsibilities to society, research subjects, and peers. Additional didactic ethics courses are included in the later semesters of the psychology programs.[130]

The Bushmaster program, which explores military contingency medicine, exposes medical and some nursing students to operationally current, reality-based missions and operational problems.[137] "Operation Bushmaster enables the military student to balance their obligations between commanders' objectives, mission accomplishment, and tactical management/execution of combat causality care."[134] The Combat Casualty Care Course (C4), conducted by the Defense Medical Readiness Training Institute, is the field training equivalent of Bushmaster for health care professionals who do not attend USUHS and also includes scenarios involving ethical decision making. Health care professionals indicated that including challenging medical ethics scenarios in realistic pre-deployment and periodic training was beneficial for both line and medical personnel.

Each Military Department provides Service-specific training in ethics (including Guard and Reserve) on accession, although this training is focused primarily on avoiding/preventing fraud, waste, and abuse, Geneva Conventions, and the Law of War/Law of Armed Conflict. The Subcommittee requested information from the Military Departments on medical ethics training for health care professionals. Each of the Services provided responses which indicated that ethics training opportunities are available in a number of courses and all indicated some level of medical ethics training is included as part of staff training at assigned medical facilities.

Continuing Education

In addition to formal education, continuing education (CE) programs offer a variety of ethics courses to military health care professionals. The Joint Medical Executive Skills Institute, a Center of Excellence in leadership development and lifelong learning, provides military members with a number of web-based continuing education courses in ethics. Course offerings include Bioethics One: Concepts and Principles, Bioethics Two: Applications, Ethical Decision Making, Leadership: Personal and Professional Ethics Decision-based Module, and Personal and Professional Ethics.

An annual health care ethics symposium is held at Walter Reed National Military Medical Center (WRNMMC). For 23 years the symposium has brought together the Walter Reed-Bethesda Ethics Committee and the Department of Pastoral Care to provide education and training. Designed to raise awareness and interest in medical ethics, the program also aims to increase attendees' competence in addressing ethical issues they might encounter. Formatted as a combination of lectures, case studies, and discussion, the symposium addresses leading ethical challenges in addition to covering "ethical theory, ethical principles, and emerging areas of clinical ethical controversy."[138] In addition to hosting the symposium, WRNMMC also holds the Medical Ethics Short Course, which focuses more specifically on training. Sponsored by the Navy Medicine Professional Development Center, the course also provides CE credits and maintains the following learning objectives:

1) Be able to recognize ethical concerns in the care of patients.
2) Recognize ethical issues when they arise in practice.
3) Have a better understanding of the proposed prioritization of health care.
4) Be able to identify moral distress in oneself and in other health care professionals.
5) Have a better understanding of and ability to assess multi-faith/cultural responses in the delivery of health care.
6) Better appreciate the crisis for health care at the end of life.[139]

While these and other medical ethics courses are not part of a formalized and required curriculum, many State health care licensing bodies require specific CE hours in ethics.[140]

As military health care professionals maintain State-issued licenses, such courses may be an individual requirement.

More specific military health care ethical issues are addressed in training on the Law of Armed Conflict (LOAC). Each Military Department is mandated to provide LOAC training, both at Service schools and during pre-deployment orientations. "Military members are informed of their obligation under the Geneva Conventions and the Uniformed Code of Military justice to provide humane treatment to all POWs [prisoners of war], retained personnel, and protected persons. Furthermore, they are informed of the nature of unlawful orders and their obligations when an unlawful order has been given."[136]

The method of ethical education and training used by the British military serves as a potential model for the Department of Defense (DoD) (Figure 5). The group-based, mandatory pre-deployment training provides a real-world decision making method for Service members to dissect ethical dilemmas. This training not only exposes Service members to real examples of ethical dilemmas, but also helps them to socialize as a team to develop trust and create a support network. Additionally, the training encourages Service members to identify contacts who may provide support in the event that they encounter an ethical challenge in the future. The Subcommittee noted that this trust is an essential aspect of ethical support infrastructure.

> The British military provides structured medical ethics training for Service members. Underwritten by the British Red Cross, an ethics symposium has been held annually since 2010, at which personnel that will be deploying to the Level-3 Field Hospital at Camp Bastion are prepared for the ethical situations they might encounter. The ethical system taught is focused on four quadrants, including medical indications, patient preferences, contextual features, and quality of life. Service members recently returned from deployment also attend to participate in the discussion of various ethical scenarios. When confronted with difficult time-critical ethical decisions, senior clinicians learn to briefly huddle in order to review the key issues of the case and attempt to achieve consensus before taking action.
>
> With the military engagement in Afghanistan drawing down, research is currently ongoing to capture the ethical challenges faced by senior hospital physicians to inform future military operations. Additionally, with the emergence of the Ebola epidemic in Western Africa additional material is being included in the symposium to address the following:
>
> 1) Rules of admission or Medical Rules of Eligibility.
> 2) The level of treatment to be provided and the rationale for decisions made.
> 3) The ethical issues around field research during a global health crisis and what research areas they are and are not prepared to support.
> 4) The ethical frictions of whether sick British personnel would be repatriated and to where.

Figure 5. Case Study: The British Military Medical Ethics Model.

Pre-deployment Training to Enhance Unit Cohesion

In meeting with Subcommittee members, some active duty Service members who are health care professionals described challenges in deploying as individuals, without the opportunity to train or bond with their unit prior to deployment. The Professional Filler System is used by the Military

Departments to fill in personnel gaps when a unit deploys. Typically, these gaps are associated with specialized positions, such as physicians, who are not permanently assigned to units due to the high personnel cost. As ethical training opportunities reported by Service members varied greatly, deploying as individuals could lead to a wide range of ethical training in a particular unit. Some Service members also noted that by simply filling in on deployments as an individual and not training with their unit, they miss the opportunity to build trust with the rest of the unit. This lack of trust could influence an individual's ability to evaluate complex ethical situations with other members of their unit.

5.3. Findings and Recommendations

Finding 13
When Service members simply fill in slots on deployments as an individual and do not train with their unit, they miss an opportunity through the training environment to establish relationships and build trust with members of their unit prior to deployment. This could make resolution of medical ethical conflicts that occur more challenging in the deployed environment.

Recommendation 13
To minimize isolation of health care professionals, the Military Departments should make every effort to ensure personnel who are deploying to the same location train together as a team prior to deployment. Establishing relationships prior to deployment may enable better communication and trust among line command and health care professionals in the deployed setting.

Finding 14
Medical ethics education and training appear to vary among Military Departments and specialties. DoD would benefit from having a common baseline education and training requirement in medical ethics across the Military Departments to ensure a consistent understanding and approach to medical ethics challenges.

Recommendation 14

DoD should issue a directive or instruction designating minimum requirements for basic and continuing education and training in military medical ethics for all health care professionals in all components and indicate the appropriate times in career progression that these should occur.

Finding 15

In recognition that health care professionals will come from different education and training backgrounds, personnel preparing for deployment would benefit from a pre-deployment review of key ethics challenges, reminders of available support tools and information, and provision of contact information for resources that might be of assistance should an ethical challenge rise. Health care professionals indicated that including challenging medical ethics scenarios in realistic pre-deployment and periodic training was beneficial for both line and medical personnel.

Recommendation 15

To enhance ethics training for military health care professionals and the line command, DoD should:

a) Ensure pre-deployment and periodic field training includes challenging medical ethics scenarios and reminders of available resources and contact information to prepare both health care professionals and line personnel. Curricula should include simulations and case studies in addition to didactics.
b) Provide a mechanism to ensure scenarios and training curricula are continually updated to reflect specific challenges and lessons learned through debriefing from real-world deployments and garrison operations.
c) Ensure key personnel returning from deployment who have faced significant challenges provide feedback to assist personnel preparing for deployment.

Finding 16

Joint Knowledge Online provides a Basic and Advanced Course in Medical Ethics and Detainee Health Care Operations. These courses provide valuable information for deploying health care professionals on ethical issues related to the care of detainees. The current implementation of the course could be improved to provide more efficient communication of the concepts and scenarios covered. In addition, it would be beneficial to have a course covering basic principles of medical ethics for all health care professionals.

Recommendation 16
To enhance health care practices in the military operational environment, DoD should:

a) Update the Joint Knowledge Online Medical Ethics and Detainee Health Care Operations courses to improve the efficiency with which the information is communicated and maintain currency of the material.
b) Create a medical ethics course to cover key principles, ethical codes, and case studies applicable to both garrison and deployed environments, in addition to providing resources and appropriate steps to take when assistance is needed in resolving complex ethical issues. This course should be required for all health care professionals.

6. CONCLUSION: THE NEED FOR A SYSTEMS APPROACH TO MILITARY MEDICAL ETHICS PREPARATION AND PRACTICE

The mission of the Department of Defense (DoD) is to provide the military forces needed to deter war and to protect the security of our country.[141] War creates an environment that continually presents challenges for which no clear ethical choice may be apparent and in which participants face extreme physical and psychological pressures. With each conflict, new lessons are learned and old ones relearned, often when leadership at some level fails to ensure that a responsible, accountable, and ethical culture is established and maintained.

Throughout the history of the United States, all branches of the military have continually endeavored to develop and abide by honorable and ethical standards and principles in the preparation for and conduct of war. DoD as an organization has to balance its absolute obligation to defend the Nation with the obligation to do so in the most ethical manner possible. Over the past decade, DoD has taken action in response to concerns regarding ethical issues to improve its policies and training. Oversight, conduct, and training for detainee operations have improved. Scenarios involving challenging ethical decisions have been incorporated into pre-deployment training exercises. Ethical principles have been emphasized in professional development courses for enlisted, non-commissioned officers, and officers. However, there is room for improvement, as suggested by the recommendations provided in this report.

Based on its review of current policies and practices across the Department, the Subcommittee identified many efforts already under way within DoD and the Military Departments to promote ethical conduct in the health care setting. However, DoD does not have an enterprise-wide, formal, integrated infrastructure to systematically build, support, sustain, and promote an evolving ethical culture within the military health care environment. Creating a comprehensive ethics infrastructure within the Military Health System could foster and inform ethical conduct in health care and could serve to lessen, mitigate, or assist in resolving ethical conflicts that might arise among health care professionals or between health care professionals and line leadership.

This perspective is consistent with the outcome of an Institute of Medicine workshop in 2008, *Military Medical Ethics: Issues Regarding Dual Loyalties*.[2] It was noted in the workshop report that improved organizational structures, systems, training, and procedures were needed so individual health professionals would not have to "act heroically" to make ethically proper decisions. Communication among the patient, provider, and commander was acknowledged as having an important role in mitigating ethical issues. There was also an emphasis on transparency and continued dialogue between the military and civilian medical communities in areas of concern. However, in attempting to find common ground, the report acknowledged the importance of ensuring that national security issues are addressed.

6.1. Response to the Charge

In addition to the findings and recommendations offered in this report, the Subcommittee offers the following summary of key aspects of the responses to the two questions posed by the Assistant Secretary of Defense for Health Affairs in the request for this report.

> How can military medical professionals most appropriately balance their obligations to their patients against their obligations as military officers to help commanders maintain military readiness?

As described in this report, military health care professionals can rely on ethics guidance and standards developed by their professional societies to guide difficult ethical decisions. These codes provide a solid foundation on which to base ethical decision making, and the elements described in the codes are remarkably consistent across the professions. In addition, DoD and Military Department policies, instructions, manuals, and standard operating procedures provide comprehensive and often detailed procedural guidance that implicitly operationalize many of the ethical principles expressed in professional codes. As noted in Section 3 of this report, there are some unique circumstances that military health care professionals might encounter in the course of their career, particularly in the combat environment. Thus, the Subcommittee recommends that DoD work to incorporate the common features of existing ethical codes and augment them with principles of special significance to military personnel, creating a military code of medical ethics.

Further, the Subcommittee found that *a priori* education and training provide the best strategies for providing military health care professionals with the skills, experience, and knowledge they can draw on when confronting difficult ethical choices. Consideration of plausible scenarios, combined with knowledge of existing codes of ethics and DoD policies, plus the opportunity to discuss the relevant issues *before* being in the heat of a situation will provide health care professionals with the working knowledge needed to make the best choice possible, given the circumstances. DoD must ensure that such education and training is available and that resources are available on an ongoing basis for personnel to seek help and information online or though consultations. Following deployment, DoD must provide means for health care professionals to acknowledge and resolve moral injuries they might have experienced during deployment.

> How much latitude should military medical professionals be given to refuse participation in medical procedures or request excusal from military operations with which they have ethical reservations or disagreement?

As described in Section 3 of this report, most organizations representing health care professionals have a code of medical ethics by which members of that profession are expected to adhere. State medical boards have standards of professional conduct that must be maintained as a condition of licensure. Many State laws also permit health care providers to invoke a conscience clause by which they may refuse to perform a legal role or responsibility based on moral or other personal objections. The Subcommittee notes that if the operation is illegal, every military member of every specialty has an obligation to do all in his or her power to stop it or refuse participation.

If a medical procedure is immoral or unethical according to the standards of the health care professional's belief system, then the senior medical officer should seek another similarly qualified professional to replace the individual who objects to the procedure.

If a medical procedure is considered unethical according to the any of the various systems that apply, then concerned parties need to resolve the conflict as time and circumstances allow before proceeding with an action. If resolution is not possible, opposing views should be given to the commander who must make the final decision regarding military operational readiness. Conflicts should be resolved through the medical chain of authority and/or military chain of command. As recommended in **Section 3** of this report, DoD leadership, particularly the line commands, should excuse health care professionals from performing medical procedures that violate their professional code of ethics, State medical board standards of conduct, or the core tenets of their religious or moral beliefs. However, to maintain morale and discipline, this excusal should not result in an individual being relieved from participating in hardship duty. Additionally, health care professionals should not be excused from military operations for which they have ethical reservations when their primary role is to care for the military members participating in those operations.

APPENDIX A: LETTER OF REQUEST

UNDER SECRETARY OF DEFENSE
4000 DEFENSE PENTAGON
WASHINGTON, DC 20301-4000

JAN 29 2013

PERSONNEL AND
READINESS

MEMORANDUM FOR PRESIDENT, DEFENSE HEALTH BOARD

SUBJECT: Request to the Defense Health Board to Review Ethical Guidelines and Practices for U.S. Military Medical Professionals

The Assistant Secretary of Defense for Health Affairs (ASD(HA)) signed a memorandum dated May 25, 2011, requesting the Defense Health Board (DHB) review military medical professional practice policies and guidelines. There are unique challenges faced by military medical professionals in their dual-hatted positions as a military officer and a medical provider. Such positions require them to balance and prioritize their role as an officer in the military and their role as a medical professional with ethical responsibilities to their patients. The following two questions from the ASD(HA) need to be reviewed and addressed by the Board:

- How can military medical professionals most appropriately balance their obligations to their patients against their obligations as military officers to help commanders maintain military readiness?
- How much latitude should military medical professionals be given to refuse participation in medical procedures or request excusal from military operations with which they have ethical reservations or disagreement?

The original request from the ASD(HA) on these two issues to be addressed by the DHB is attached. Provide a response on these items to the ASD(HA).

Jessica L. Wright
Acting

Attachment:
As stated

cc:
ASD(HA)

APPENDIX B: TERMS OF REFERENCE

These terms of reference establish the objectives for the Defense Health Board's (DHB) review of ethical guidelines and practices for military medical professionals within the Department of Defense (DoD). They outline the scope and methodology of DHB's examination in responding to DoD's request.

Mission Statement: To conduct a comprehensive review of current military medical professional practice policies and guidelines and recommend a strategy for DoD to optimally support military medical professionals as they confront ethical dilemmas.

Issue Statement: As health care professionals, military medical professionals have ethical responsibilities to their patients, which arise from a variety of legal, moral, and professional codes as well as personal moral and religious beliefs of both the caregiver and the patient. However, military health care professionals must balance and prioritize these ethical responsibilities with their role as a military officer.

On January 29, 2013, the Acting Under Secretary of Defense for Personnel and Readiness endorsed a request that the DHB examine the challenges military medical professionals face in their dual role as medical providers and military officers, and provide recommendations on how they may best balance these roles and to what extent they should be allowed to withdraw from participating in activities on ethical grounds.

Objectives and Scope: The DHB will address the following questions in its report, and provide a recommended strategy for DoD to address the following questions of dual loyalties of medical providers in DoD:

1) How can military medical professionals most appropriately balance their obligations to their patients against their obligations as military officers to help commanders maintain military readiness?
2) How much latitude should military medical professionals be given to refuse participation in medical procedures or request excusal from military operations with which they have ethical reservations or disagreement?

Methodology: The Medical Ethics Subcommittee will review current civilian and military medical professional practice policies and guidelines as well as medical ethics education and training within DoD and leading civilian institutions. As needed, members will conduct interviews with and receive briefings from subject matter experts and DoD personnel including Active Duty, Guard, Reserve, and retired military medical professionals and line officers. The members will review the literature and information received from briefings, conduct site visits as needed, and present their preliminary findings and recommendations to the DHB for consideration and deliberation. The DHB will deliberate the findings and recommendations proposed by the Subcommittee, making revisions as deemed necessary, and vote on the final version in an open public session.

Deliverable: Upon achieving majority consensus on the report content and specific findings and recommendations, the DHB will produce the final report immediately following approval for presentation to DoD. The Subcommittee will provide progress updates to the Board at each DHB meeting until the report is finalized.

Membership: The Medical Ethics Subcommittee members will conduct the primary review and will consult subject matter experts as needed.

Support:
1) The DHB office will provide any necessary administrative, analytical, research and logistical support for the Board.
2) Funding for this review is included in the DHB operating budget.

APPENDIX C: MEETINGS AND BRIEFINGS

August 20, 2013
Annapolis, Maryland
At this meeting, members discussed the tasking and relevant publications and subject matter experts. There were no briefings at this meeting.

November 7, 2013
Falls Church, Virginia
Members met with subject matter experts to discuss dual loyalties and ethical conflicts.
Subject matter experts in attendance included:

- Dr. Sondra Crosby, Associate Professor of Medicine, Boston University
- Dr. Edmund Howe, Uniformed Services University of the Health Sciences, Department of Psychiatry
- Dr. W. Brad Johnson, Professor of Psychology, Department of Leadership, Ethics & Law, U.S. Naval Academy
- Dr. Warren Lockette, Former Deputy Assistant Secretary of Defense for Clinical and Program Policy
- Mr. Jonathan Marks, Associate Professor of Bioethics, Humanities, Law and Philosophy, Pennsylvania State University
- Dr. Albert Pierce, Professor of Ethics and National Security, National Defense University
- Dr. Jonathan Woodson, Assistant Secretary of Defense for Health Affairs

December 9, 2013
On this teleconference, members discussed potential site visits and briefers.

January 14, 2014
On this teleconference, members reviewed the Terms of Reference, Guiding Principles, and relevant reference materials. Members also discussed future meetings and briefers.

February 26, 2014
Falls Church, Virginia

Members met with Trauma and Injury Subcommittee members and Department of Defense health care professionals to discuss dual loyalties and ethical conflicts.

March 10, 2014
Ft. Bragg, North Carolina

Members met with Service members to discuss dual loyalties and ethical conflicts.

March 31, 2014
On this teleconference, members finalized the Terms of Reference and Guiding Principles. Members also discussed future meetings and the way forward.

April 24, 2014
On this teleconference, members discussed dual loyalties and ethical conflicts with a subject matter expert, BG (Ret.) Stephen Xenakis, a former U.S. Army Medical Corps Officer. Members also finalized the Terms of Reference and Guiding Principles and reviewed the draft report outline and report writing plan.

June 16, 2014
Falls Church, Virginia
Members met with subject matter experts to discuss dual loyalties and ethical conflicts.
Subject matter experts in attendance included:

- Dr. Thomas Beam, The Center for Bioethics & Human Dignity
- LTG (Ret.) Ronald Blanck, Chairman, Martin, Blanck & Associates
- Dr. Leonard Rubenstein, Senior Scholar and Director of the Program in Human Rights, Health, and Conflict
- Dr. Laura Sessums, Director, Division of Advanced Primary Care, Centers for Medicare & Medicaid Services
- CAPT (Ret.) Albert Shimkus, U.S. Naval War College, National Security Affairs

September 8, 2014 Falls Church, Virginia

Members met with subject matter experts to discuss dual loyalties and ethical conflicts.

Subject matter experts in attendance included:

- Ms. Laurie Badzek, Director, Center for Ethics and Human Rights, American Nurses Association
- Dr. Stephen Behnke, Director of Ethics, American Psychological Association, Appointment Clinical Ethics; Department of Psychiatry at Harvard Medical School; Chair, Board of Directors, Saks Institute for Mental Health Law, Policy, and Ethics, University of Southern California Law School
- CAPT Stephen Bree, British Liaison Officer (Deployment Health), Military Health system; United Kingdom Royal Navy
- Dr. Stephen Brotherton, Texas Health Care Bone and Joint Clinic; President, Texas Medical Association; Member, American Medical Association, Council on Ethical and Judicial Affairs
- CAPT Roosevelt Brown, Chaplain of Navy Medicine, Pastoral Care Office, Bureau of Medicine and Surgery
- Col William Dunn, U.S. Air Force Chief, USAF Dental Evaluation and Consultation Service, Institute for Surgical Research, Battlefield Health and Trauma-2
- COL Jonathan Fruendt, Deputy Chief, Clinical Policy Services, U.S. Army Medical Command
- Dr. Cecil Wilson, Immediate Past President, World Medical Association, Past President, American Medical Association

October 16, 2014

Bethesda, Maryland

Members met via teleconference with members of the ethics committees from Walter Reed National Military Medical Center, Portsmouth Naval Hospital, and Naval Medical Center San Diego to discuss dual loyalties and ethical conflicts.

November 20, 2014

On this teleconference, members discussed dual loyalties and ethical conflicts with a subject matter expert, Col (Ret.) Schuyler Geller. Members also discussed and reviewed the draft report.

December 2, 2014
Washington, D.C.
Members met with Service members from the National Guard and Reserve to discuss dual loyalties and ethical conflicts.

December 11, 2014
On this teleconference, members discussed and reviewed the draft report. There were no briefings at this meeting.

January 6, 2015
On this teleconference, members discussed and reviewed the draft report. There were no briefings at this meeting.

January 20, 2015
On this teleconference, members discussed and reviewed the draft report. There were no briefings at this meeting.

January 29, 2015
On this teleconference, members discussed and reviewed the draft report. There were no briefings at this meeting.

February 3, 2015
On this teleconference, members discussed and reviewed the draft report. There were no briefings at this meeting.

February 11, 2015
Defense Health Board Meeting Falls Church, Virginia
Dr. Adil Shamoo, Subcommittee chair, presented the deliberative predecisional draft of the report.

APPENDIX D: FUNDAMENTAL ETHICAL THEORIES AND EXCERPTS FROM SELECTED CODES OF ETHICS

Principles of medical ethics rest on several ethical theories or approaches for considering moral dilemmas. Teleological approaches, such as utilitarianism, emphasize the importance of evaluating the consequences (good and bad) of actions as the first consideration when facing a moral dilemma.

The approach holds that one should choose the action or policy that is likely to have the most positive overall outcome.[142] It is sometimes characterized as making choices that will provide "the greatest good for the greatest number." Critics of this approach argue that one cannot always predict what the most positive outcome will be and that what is best for society might not always be best for the individual.

In comparison, deontological theories emphasize honoring one's duties and responsibilities, irrespective of the consequences. Advanced initially by German philosopher Immanuel Kant in his *Critique of Practical Reason* (1788), this theory stresses the importance of following moral rules that would be adopted by rational individuals (moral agents; in the context of this report, the health care professional serves as a moral agent). Moral rules are based on a general principle known as the categorical imperative. According to one version of this principle, one should act so that the maxim for one's action could become a universal rule. According to a different version of this principle, one should treat all people as having inherent moral value, not merely as a means to obtain some goal. Moral conduct is based on doing one's duty for duty's sake. Critics of this approach argue that it does not give sufficient consideration to evaluating the consequences of one's actions and is too absolutist because it does not allow for reasonable exceptions to moral rules.

Virtue theory emphasizes the importance of developing moral virtue and living a good life. It stresses the influence of parents, mentors, and community, asserting that moral virtues are learned through imitation and practice. It dates back to Aristotle, who argued that the purpose of mankind is to exercise virtue (or excellence). Aristotle claimed that virtues are a mean between two extremes. For example, courage is a means between cowardice (too little courage) and foolhardiness (too much courage). Critics of virtue theory say that it is too ambiguous because it does not provide specific guidance related to moral dilemmas and that it is subject to the relative values of the individual and his or her community.[143]

United Nations- Principles of Medical Ethics Relevant to the Role of Health Personnel, Particularly Physicians, in the Protection of Prisoners and Detainees against Torture and Other Cruel, Inhuman or Degrading Treatment or Punishment

Adopted by General Assembly resolution 37/194 of 18 December 1982

Principle 4

It is a contravention of medical ethics for health personnel, particularly physicians:

a) To apply their knowledge and skills in order to assist in the interrogation of prisoners and detainees in a manner that may adversely affect the physical or mental health or condition of such prisoners or detainees and which is not in accordance with the relevant international instruments;
b) To certify, or to participate in the certification of, the fitness of prisoners or detainees for any form of treatment or punishment that may adversely affect their physical or mental health and which is not in accordance with the relevant international instruments, or to participate in any way in the infliction of any such treatment or punishment which is not in accordance with the relevant international instruments.

Principle 5

It is a contravention of medical ethics for health personnel, particularly physicians, to participate in any procedure for restraining a prisoner or detainee unless such a procedure is determined in accordance with purely medical criteria as being necessary for the protection of the physical or mental health or the safety of the prisoner or detainee himself, of his fellow prisoners or detainees, or of his guardians, and presents no hazard to his physical or mental health.[144]

Principle 6

There may be no derogation from the foregoing principles on any ground whatsoever, including public emergency.[144]

American Medical Association- Opinion 2.067 – Torture

Torture refers to the deliberate, systematic, or wanton administration of cruel, inhumane, and degrading treatments or punishments during imprisonment or detainment.[145]

Physicians must oppose and must not participate in torture for any reason. Participation in torture includes, but is not limited to, providing or withholding any services, substances, or knowledge to facilitate the practice of torture. Physicians must not be present when torture is used or threatened.[145]

Physicians may treat prisoners or detainees if doing so is in their best interest, but physicians should not treat individuals to verify their health so that torture can begin or continue. Physicians who treat torture victims should not be persecuted. Physicians should help provide support for victims of torture and, whenever possible, strive to change situations in which torture is practiced or the potential for torture is great.[145] (I, III)

WMA Declaration of Malta on Hunger Strikers

Adopted by the 43rd World Medical Assembly, St. Julians, Malta, November 1991 and editorially revised by the 44th World Medical Assembly, Marbella, Spain, September 1992 and revised by the 57th WMA General Assembly, Pilanesberg, South Africa, October 2006.[146]

Preamble
1. Hunger strikes occur in various contexts but they mainly give rise to dilemmas in settings where people are detained (prisons, jails and immigration detention centres). They are often a form of protest by people who lack other ways of making their demands known. In refusing nutrition for a significant period, they usually hope to obtain certain goals by inflicting negative publicity on the authorities. Short-term or feigned food refusals rarely raise ethical problems. Genuine and prolonged fasting risks death or permanent damage for hunger strikers and can create a conflict of values for physicians. Hunger strikers usually do not wish to die but some may be prepared to do so to achieve their aims. Physicians need to ascertain the individual's true intention, especially in collective strikes or situations where peer pressure may be a factor. An ethical dilemma arises when hunger strikers who have apparently issued clear instructions not to be resuscitated reach a stage of cognitive impairment. The principle of beneficence urges physicians to resuscitate them but respect for individual autonomy restrains physicians from intervening when a valid and informed refusal has been made. An added difficulty arises in custodial settings because it is not always clear whether the hunger striker's advance instructions were made voluntarily and with appropriate information about the consequences. These guidelines and the background paper address such difficult situations.[146]

Principles

1) Duty to act ethically. All physicians are bound by medical ethics in their professional contact with vulnerable people, even when not providing therapy. Whatever their role, physicians must try to prevent coercion or maltreatment of detainees and must protest if it occurs.
2) Respect for autonomy. Physicians should respect individuals' autonomy. This can involve difficult assessments as hunger strikers' true wishes may not be as clear as they appear. Any decisions lack moral force if made involuntarily by use of threats, peer pressure or coercion. Hunger strikers should not be forcibly given treatment they refuse. Forced feeding contrary to an informed and voluntary refusal is unjustifiable. Artificial feeding with the hunger striker's explicit or implied consent is ethically acceptable.
3) 'Benefit' and 'harm'. Physicians must exercise their skills and knowledge to benefit those they treat. This is the concept of 'beneficence', which is complemented by that of 'non-maleficence' or primum non nocere. These two concepts need to be in balance. 'Benefit' includes respecting individuals' wishes as well as promoting their welfare. Avoiding 'harm' means not only minimising damage to health but also not forcing treatment upon competent people nor coercing them to stop fasting. Beneficence does not necessarily involve prolonging life at all costs, irrespective of other values.
4) Balancing dual loyalties. Physicians attending hunger strikers can experience a conflict between their loyalty to the employing authority (such as prison management) and their loyalty to patients. Physicians with dual loyalties are bound by the same ethical principles as other physicians, that is to say that their primary obligation is to the individual patient.
5) Clinical independence. Physicians must remain objective in their assessments and not allow third parties to influence their medical judgement. They must not allow themselves to be pressured to breach ethical principles, such as intervening medically for non-clinical reasons.
6) Confidentiality. The duty of confidentiality is important in building trust but it is not absolute. It can be overridden if non-disclosure seriously harms others. As with other patients, hunger strikers' confidentiality should be respected unless they agree to disclosure or unless information sharing is necessary to prevent serious harm. If

individuals agree, their relatives and legal advisers should be kept informed of the situation.
7) Gaining trust. Fostering trust between physicians and hunger strikers is often the key to achieving a resolution that both respects the rights of the hunger strikers and minimises harm to them. Gaining trust can create opportunities to resolve difficult situations. Trust is dependent upon physicians providing accurate advice and being frank with hunger strikers about the limitations of what they can and cannot do, including where they cannot guarantee confidentiality.[146]

APPENDIX E: ACRONYMS

AAPA	American Academy of Physician Assistants
ACIP	Advisory Committee on Immunization Practices
ACOG	American College of Gynecologists and Obstetricians
AFTH	Air Force Theater Hospital
AMA	American Medical Association
AMEDD	United States Army Medical Department
ANA	American Nurses Association
ASBH	American Society for Bioethics + Humanities
ASD(HA)	Assistant Secretary of Defense for Health Affairs
C4	Combat Casualty Care Course
CDC	Centers for Disease Control and Prevention
CFR	Code of Federal Regulations
CoC	Code of Conduct
DHB	Defense Health Board
DNA	Deoxyribonucleic acid
DoD	Department of Defense
DoDD	Department of Defense Direction
DoDI	Department of Defense Instruction
DOS	Department of State
EMEDS	Expeditionary Medical Support
FDA	Food and Drug Administration
FDR	Foreign disaster relief
FHA	Foreign humanitarian assistance
FSMC	Forward support medical company

HA/DR	Humanitarian assistance/disaster relief
HCEC	Health care ethics consultation
HIPAA	Health Insurance Portability and Accountability Act
HIS	International health specialist
IND	Investigational new drug
JP	Joint Publication
LOAC	Law of armed conflict
MC	Medical Corps
MHS	Military Health System
MTF	Military Treatment Facility
NGO	Non-governmental organization
POW	Prisoner of war
PROFIS	Professional Filler System
TFC	Tactical field care
TOE	Tables of Organization and Equipment
U.S.	United States
USAID	United States Agency for International Development
USD(P&R)	Under Secretary of Defense for Personnel and Readiness
USUHS	Uniformed Services University of the Health Sciences
VA	Department of Veterans Affairs
VHA	Veterans Health Administration
VUCA	Volatility, uncertainty, complexity, and ambiguity
WMA	World Medical Association
WRNMMC	Walter Reed National Military Medical Center

APPENDIX F: SUPPORT STAFF

Allen Middleton, S.E.S.
Deputy Director, Defense Health Agency
Former Deputy Assistant Secretary of Defense
for Health Budgets and Financial Policy/
Defense Health Board Designated Federal Officer

Christine Bader, M.S., B.S.N., R.N.-B.C.
Defense Health Board Director and Independent
Review Panel on Military Medical Construction Standards

Col Douglas Rouse, M.C., S.F.S.
Defense Health Board Executive Secretary
(starting August 2013)

Camille Gaviola, M.B.A.
Defense Health Board Deputy Director and Independent Review Panel on Military Medical Construction Standards

Kathi E. Hanna, M.S., Ph.D.
Lead Writer, Creative Computing Solutions, Inc. (CCSi)

Lisa Austin, MSHA, MBA
Task Lead, Grant Thornton, LLP

Elizabeth Ribeiro, M.S.P.H., C.P.H.
Analyst, CCSi
(Until January 2015)

Sara Higgins M.P.H.
Analyst, Grant Thornton, LLP

Ariel Markowitz-Shulman, M.S.
Analyst, Grant Thornton, LLP

Marianne Coates
Communications Advisor, CCSi

Kendal Brown, M.B.A.
Management Analyst, CCSi

Margaret Welsh
Event Manager, Grant Thornton, LLP

Jean Ward
Defense Health Board Staff Assistant

Report References

[1] Beam TE, Sparacino LR, eds. *Military Medical Ethics*. Washington, DC: Office of the Surgeon General U.S. Army, Borden Institute, Walter Reed Army Medical Center; 2003. Pellegrino ED, Hartle AE, Howe EG, eds.

[2] Institute of Medicine Board on Health Sciences Policy. *Military Medical Ethics: Issues Regarding Dual Loyalties: Workshop Summary*. Washington, DC: National Academies Press; 2008.

[3] Clark PA. Medical ethics at Guantanamo Bay and Abu Ghraib: The problem of dual loyalty. *The Journal of Law, Medicine & Ethics*. 2006;34(3):570-580, 481.

[4] London L, Rubenstein LS, Baldwin-Ragaven L, Van Es A. Dual loyalty among military health professionals: human rights and ethics in times of armed conflict. *Camb. Q. Healthc. Ethics*. Fall 2006;15(4):381-391.

[5] Malke B. Ethical dilemmas for physicians in time of war. *Isr. Med. Assoc. J.* Mar 2010;12(3):172-173.

[6] Williams J. Dual loyalties: how to resolve ethical conflict. *The South African Journal of Bioethics & Law*. 2009;2(1).

[7] Allhoff F. Physicians at War: The Dual-Loyalties Challenge. In: Allhoff F, ed. *Physicians at War*. Vol 41: Springer Netherlands; 2008:3-11.

[8] U.S. Department of the Army. Oath of Office - Military Personnel. *DA Form 71*1999.

[9] Martin C, Vaught W, Solomon RC. *Ethics Across the Professions: A Reader for Professional Ethics*. Oxford: Oxford University Press; 2009.

[10] Fox EF, Crigger B, Bottrell M, Bauck P. *Ethical Leadership: Fostering an Ethical Environment & Culture*. National Center for Ethics in Health Care, Veterans Health Administration.

[11] Robbins SP, Judge TA. *Organizational Behavior* 13th ed. Upper Saddle River, NJ: Pearson Education, Inc.; 2009.

[12] Coleman S. *Military Ethics: An Introduction with Case Studies*. Oxford University Press; 2012.

[13] Beauchamp TL, Childress JF. *Principles of Biomedical Ethics*. Seventh ed: Oxford University Press; 2012.

[14] American Medical Association. AMA's Code of Medical Ethics. 2001.

[15] World Medical Association. WMA Declaration of Geneva. 1994.

[16] American Nurses Association. Code of Ethics for Nurses with Interpretive Statements. Silver Spring, MD: Nursebooks.org; 2015.

[17] World Medical Association. International Code of Medical Ethics. 2006.

[18] Pauly BM, Varcoe C, Storch J. Framing the issues: moral distress in health care. *HEC Forum*. 2012;24(1):1-11.

[19] Visser SL. The Soldier and Autonomy. In: Sparacino LR, Pellegrino ED, eds. *Military Medical Ethics*. Vol 1. Washington, DC: Office of the Surgeon General U.S. Army, Borden Institute, Walter Reed Army Medical Center; 2003:251-266.

[20] Singh JA. Military tribunals at Guantanamo Bay: dual loyalty conflicts. *Lancet*. Aug 16 2003;362(9383):573.

[21] Singh JA. American physicians and dual loyalty obligations in the "war on terror". *BMC medical ethics*. Aug 1 2003;4:E4.

[22] Kelly J. Battlefield conditions: different environment but the same duty of care. *Nurs. Ethics*. Sep 2010;17(5):636-645.

[23] Benatar SR, Upshur REG. Dual loyalty of physicians in the military and in civilian life. *Am. J. Public Health.* 2008;98(12).
[24] International Committee of the Red Cross. Convention (I) for the Amelioration of the Condition of the Wounded and Sick in Armed Forces in the Field. *Article 22* 1949.
[25] WMA Regulations in Times of Armed Conflict and Other Situations of Violence. In: World Medical Association, ed2012.
[26] Ramsey P. *The Patient as Person: Exploration in Medical Ethics.* Second ed. New Haven, CT: Yale University Press; 2002.
[27] Johnson CE. *Organizational Ethics: a Practical Approach.* Second ed: SAGE Publications, Inc.; 2012.
[28] Fletcher JF. *Morals and medicine.* Princeton, NJ: Princeton University Press; 1954.
[29] Siegler M. Clinical ethics and clinical medicine. *Arch. Intern. Med.* 1979;139(8):914-915.
[30] WMA Declaration of Helsinki - Ethical Priciples for Medical Research Involving Human Subjects. In: World Medical Association, ed2013.
[31] The National Commission for the Protection of Human Subjects of Biomedical and Behavioral Research. *The Belmont Report: Ethical Principles and Guidelines for the Protection of Human Subjects of Research.* Washington, DC 1978. DHEW Publication OS 78-0012.
[32] Rascona DR. Physician-soldier: A Moral Dilemma? In: Sparacino LR, Pellegrino ED, eds. *Military Medical Ethics.* Vol 1. Washington, DC: Office of the Surgeon General U.S. Army, Borden Institute, Walter Reed Army Medical Center; 2003:320-325.
[33] Maguen S, Litz B. Moral injury in veterans of war. *PTSD Research Quarterly.* 2012;23(1):1050-1835.
[34] Litz BT, Stein N, Delaney E, et al. Moral injury and moral repair in war veterans: a preliminary model and intervention strategy. *Clin. Psychol. Rev.* 2009;29(8):695-706.
[35] Madden W, Carter BS. Physician-soldier: A Moral Profession. In: Sparacino LR, Pellegrino ED, eds. *Military Medical Ethics.* Vol 1. Washington, DC: Office of the Surgeon General U.S. Army, Borden Institute, Walter Reed Army Medical Center; 2003:269-291.
[36] American Medical Association. Principles of Medical Ethics. 2001.
[37] American Medical Association. Declaration of Professional Responsibility. San Francisco, CA2001.
[38] American Psychiatric Association. The Principles of Medical Ethics with Annotations Especially Applicable to Psychiatry. 2013.
[39] American Psychological Association. Ethical Principles of Psychologists and Code of Conduct. 2010.
[40] American Academy of Physicians Assistants. Guidelines for Ethical Conduct for the Physician Assistant Profession. 2013.
[41] American Osteopathic Association. AOA code of ethics. 2015; http://www.osteopathic.org/inside-aoa/about/leadership/Pages/aoa-code-of-ethics.aspx. Accessed January 30, 2015.
[42] Health Systems Research Inc., An Altarum company. *Mass Medical Care with Scarce esources: a Community Planning Guide.* Prepared for the Agency for Healthcare Research and Quality 2007.
[43] World Medical Association. WMA Declaration of Tokyo - Guidelines for Physicians Concerning Torture and other Cruel, Inhuman or Degrading Treatment or Punishment in Relation to Detention and Imprisonment. 2006.
[44] Physicians for Human Rights and School of Public Health and Primary Health Care. *Dual Loyalty & Human Rights: In Health Professional Practices; Proposed Guidelines & Institutional Mechanisms.* University of Cape Town, Health Sciences Faculty;2002.

[45] American Medical Association. AMA Code of Medical Ethics. *Opinion 2.068 -Physician Participation in Interrogation* 2006.
[46] Snyder L. American College of Physicians Ethics Manual Sixth Edition. *Ann. Intern. Med.* 2012;156(1_Part_2):73-104.
[47] Behnke S. Ethics and interrogations: comparing and contrasting the American Psychological, American Medical and American Psychiatric Association positions. *Monitor on Psychology.* 2006;37(7):66.
[48] American Psychological Association. Timeline of APA policies & actions related to detainee welfare and professional ethics in the context of interrogation and national security. http://www.apa.org/news/press/statements/interrogations.aspx. Accessed December 18, 2014.
[49] American Nurses Association. Force-feeding of detainees at Guantanamo Bay. http://www.nursingworld.org/MainMenuCategories/EthicsStandards/Resources/Force-feeding-of-Detainees-at-Guantanamo-Bay.html. Accessed January 26, 2015.
[50] U.S. Bureau of Prisons. Hunger Strikes, Inmate. *28 CFR Part 549, Subpart E.*
[51] Feinstein D. In: Hagel C, ed. Washington, DC: U.S. Senate Select Committee on Intelligence; 2013.
[52] Guttmacher Institute. *Refusing to Provide Health Services.* 2014.
[53] American Congress of Obstetricians and Gynecologists. The limits of conscientious refusal in reproductive medicine ACOG Opinion no.385. *Obstet. Gynecol.* 2007;110:1203-1208.
[54] Harvey JC. Clinical Ethics: The Art of Medicine. In: Sparacino LR, Pellegrino ED, eds. *Military Medical Ethics.* Vol 1. Washington, DC: Office of the Surgeon General U.S. Army, Borden Institute, Walter Reed Army Medical Center; 2003:61-104.
[55] In re Quinlan, 70 NJ. 10, 355 A.2d 647 (NJ. 1976). *cert. denied sub. nom. Garger v. New Jersey, 429 U.S. 922* 1976.
[56] American Medical Association. AMA Code of Medical Ethics. *Opinion 9.115 - Ethics Consultations* 1998.
[57] American Society for Bioethics and Humanities. Code of Ethics and Professional Responsibilities for Healthcare Ethics Consultants. 2014.
[58] American Society for Bioethics and Humanities. Core Competencies for Healthcare Ethics Consultations. Second edition. Glenview, IL: American Society for Bioethics and Humanities; 2011.
[59] Fox E, Myers S, Pearlman RA. Ethics consultation in United States hospitals: a national survey. *The American Journal of Bioethics.* 2007;7(2):13-25.
[60] O'Reilly KB. Willing, but waiting: hospital ethics committees. 2008; http://www.amednews.com/article/20080128/profession/301289970/4/. Accessed January 30, 2015.
[61] Orlowski JP, Hein S, Christensen JA, Meinke R, Sincich T. Why doctors use or do not use ethics consultation. *J. Med. Ethics.* 2006;32(9):499-503.
[62] Fox E. Developing a certifying examination for health care ethics consultants: bioethicists need help. *The American Journal of Bioethics.* 2014;14(1):1-4.
[63] American Society for Bioethics and Humanities. Code of ethics and professional responsibilities for healthcare ethics consultants. 2014.
[64] U.S. Department of Defense. *Review of the Military Health System - Final Report to the Secretary of Defense.* Washington, DC2014.
[65] U.S. Department of Veterans Affairs. National Center for Ethics in Health Care. http://www.ethics.va.gov/. Accessed December 18, 2014.

[66] Hartle AE. The Profession of Arms and the Officer Corps. In: Sparacino LR, Pellegrino ED, eds. *Military Medical Ethics.* Vol 1. Washington, DC: Office of the Surgeon General U.S. Army, Borden Institute, Walter Reed Army Medical Center; 2003:129-156.

[67] U.S. Department of Defense. Joint Ethics Regulation *5500.7-R.* 1993.

[68] U.S. Department of Defense. The Armed Forces Officer. Washington, DC 2006.

[69] Dempsey ME, Battaglia BB. *The Noncommissioned Officer and Petty Officer: Backbone of the Armed Forces.* Washington, DC: National Defense University Press; 2014.

[70] Center for the Army Profession and Ethic. The Army ethic white paper. U.S. Army Combined Arms Center 2014.

[71] Department of the Navy. Navy Code of Ethics. 2005; http://ethics.navy.mil/content/codeofethics.aspx. Accessed January 30, 2015.

[72] Janssen HG. A proposed code of ethics for Air Force officers: a common-sense approach. *Air University Review.* 1968.

[73] U.S. Department of Defense. Military code of ethics. 2005; https://kb.defense.gov/app/answers/detail/a_id/461/~/military-code-of-ethics. Accessed January 30, 2015.

[74] Kirkland FR. Honor, Combat Ethics, and Military Culture. In: Sparacino LR, Pellegrino ED, eds. *Military Medical Ethics.* Vol 1. Washington, DC: Office of the Surgeon General U.S. Army, Borden Institute, Walter Reed Army Medical Center; 2003:157-197.

[75] U.S. Joint Chiefs of Staff. Joint Publication (JP) 1, Doctrine for the Armed Forces of the United States. 2013.

[76] Woodson J. Guidance for the Use of Influenza Vaccine for the 2014-2015 Influenza Season. In: Office of the Secretary of Defense for Health Affairs, ed. Washington, DC 2014.

[77] Rettig RA. The history of the interim rule. *Military use of drugs not yet approved by the FDA for CW/BW defense: lessons from the Gulf War*: RAND Corporation; 1999.

[78] U.S. Department of Health and Human Services. Code of Federal Regulations Title 21 Section 50.23. 2014.

[79] U.S. Department of Defense. Standards of Conduct *Department of Defense Directive 5500.07.*2007.

[80] U.S. Department of Defense. Code of Conduct (CoC) Training and Education. *Department of Defense Instruction 1300.21.* Washington, DC 2001.

[81] U.S. Department of the Army. Medical Platoon Leaders' Handbook: Tactics, Techniques, and Procedures. *Field Manual 4-02.4.* 2003.

[82] U.S. Department of the Army. Division and Brigade Surgeons' Handbook. *Field Manual 4-02.21.* Washington, DC 2000.

[83] Emergency War Surgery. In: Cubano MA, Lenhart MK, eds. Fort Sam Houston, Texas: The Office of the Surgeon General, Borden Institute; 2013.

[84] National Association of Emergency Medical Technicians. *Prehospital Trauma Life Support, Military Edition.* 8 ed: Jones & Bartlett Learning; 2014.

[85] U.S. Department of Defense. Stability Operations. *Joint Publication 3-07.* Washington, DC 2011.

[86] U.S. Department of Defense. Foreign Humanitarian Assistance. *Joint Publication 3-29.* Washington, DC 2014.

[87] Office for the Coordination of Humanitarian Affairs. Oslo Guidelines: Guidelines on the Use of Foreign Military and Civil Defence Assets in Disaster Relief. 2007.

[88] U.S. Department of Defense. Sexual Assault Prevention and Response (SAPR) Program Procedures. *Department of Defense Instruction 6495.02.* Washington, DC 2013.

[89] U.S. Department of Defense. Privacy of individually identifiable health information in DoD health care programs. *Department of Defense Instruction 6025.18.* Washington, DC 2009.

[90] U.S. Department of Health and Human Services. The privacy rule. http://www.hhs.gov/ocr/privacy/hipaa/administrative/privacyrule/. Accessed January 30, 2015.

[91] U.S. Department of Defense. DoD Health Information Privacy Regulation. *6025.18-R.* Washington, DC 2003.

[92] U.S. Department of Defense. Mental Health Evaluation of Members of the Military Services. *Department of Defense Instruction 6490.04.* Washington, DC 2013.

[93] U.S. Department of Defense. Command Notification Requirements to Dispel Stigma in Providing Mental Health Care to Service Members. *Department of Defense Instruction 6490.08.* Washington, DC 2011.

[94] U.S. Department of Defense. Medical Program Support for Detainee Operations. *Department of Defense Instruction 2310.08E.* Washington, DC 2006.

[95] U.S. Department of Defense. *Review of Department Compliance with President's Executive Order on Detainee Conditions of Confinement.* 2009.

[96] Joint Task Force Guantanamo Bay Cuba Joint Medical Group. Medical management of detainees on hunger strike. *Standard Operating Procedure JTF-JMG #001*2013.

[97] U.S. Department of Defense. Detainee Operations. *Joint Publication 3-63.* Washington, DC 2008.

[98] Care of Enemy Prisoners of War/Internees. In: Cubano MA, Lenhart MK, eds. *Emergency war surgery.* Vol Fourth United States Revision. Fort Sam Houston, Texas: The Office of the Surgeon General, Borden Institute:461-466.

[99] International Committee of the Red Cross. Protocol (I) Additional to the Geneva Conventions of 12 August 1949, and relating to the Protection of Victims of International Armed Conflicts. Geneva, Switzerland 1977.

[100] International Committee of the Red Cross. Protocol (II) Additional to the Geneva Conventions of 12 August 1949, and relating to the Protection of Victims of Non-International Armed Conflicts. Geneva, Switzerland 1977.

[101] U.S. Department of Defense. Health Service Support. *Joint Publication 4-02.* Washington, DC 2012.

[102] Sessums LL, Collen JF, O'Malley PG, Jackson JL, Roy MJ. Ethical practice under fire: deployed physicians in the global war on terrorism. *Mil. Med.* 2009;174(5):441-447.

[103] Adams MP. Triage Priorities and Military Physicians. In: Alhoff F, ed. *Physicians at War:* Springer; 2008:215-236.

[104] Butler FK, Jr., Hagmann J, Butler EG. Tactical combat casualty care in special operations. *Mil. Med.* Aug 1996;161 Suppl:3-16.

[105] Eastridge BJ, Butler F, Wade CE, et al. Field triage score (FTS) in battlefield casualties: validation of a novel triage technique in a combat environment. *Am. J. Surg.* Dec 2010;200(6):724-727; discussion 727.

[106] Beam TE. Medical Ethics on the Battlefield: The Crucible of Military Medical Ethics. In: Beam TE, Sparacino LR, eds. *Military Medical Ethics.* Vol 2. Washington, DC: Office of the Surgeon General U.S. Army, Borden Institute, Walter Reed Army Medical Center; 2003:369-402.

[107] International Committee of the Red Cross. Convention (I) for the Amelioration of the Condition of the Wounded and Sick in Armed Forces in the Field. *Chapter II, Article 12.* Geneva, Switzerland 1949.

[108] U.S. Department of the Army. Planning for Health Service Support. *Field Manual 8-55.* Washington, DC1994.

[109] Zajtchuk JT. Military Medicine in Humanitarian Missions. In: Sparacino LR, Pellegrino ED, eds. *Military Medical Ethics*. Vol 2. Washington, DC: Office of the Surgeon General U.S. Army, Borden Institute, Walter Reed Army Medical Center; 2003:773-804.

[110] The White House. Fact sheet: U.S. response to the Ebola epidemic in West Africa. 2014; http://www.whitehouse.gov/the-press-office/2014/09/16/fact-sheet-us-response-ebola-epidemic-west-africa. Accessed January 30, 2015.

[111] Geller SK. Hearing to examine the facts and circumstances surrounding alleged corruption and mismanagement at the U.S. taxpayer-funded Dawood National Military Hospital located in Afghanistan. Subcommittee on National Security, Homeland Defense and Foreign Operations of the House Committee on Oversight and Government Reform2012.

[112] Andriacco M. U.S. Airmen help open hospital in Afghanistan. 2007; http://www.defense.gov/news/newsarticle.aspx?id=48472. Accessed January 30, 2015.

[113] Basu S. U.S. medical personnel in impossible situation mentoring at substandard Kabul hospital. 2012; http://www.usmedicine.com/agencies/department-of-defense-dod/us-medical-personnel-in-impossible-situation-mentoring-at-substandard-kabul-hospital/. Accessed January 30, 2015.

[114] U.S. Department of the Air Force. Expeditionary Medical Support (EMEDS) and Air Force Theater Hospital (AFTH). In: Secretary of the Air Force, ed. *Air Force Tactics, Techniques and Procedures 3-42.7*2014.

[115] Annas GJ. Hunger strikes at Guantanamo--medical ethics and human rights in a "legal black hole". *N. Engl. J. Med.* Sep 28 2006;355(13):1377-1382.

[116] U.S. Department of the Army Inspector General. *Detainee Operations Inspection*. Washington, DC 2004.

[117] Taguba AM. *Article 15-6 Investigation of the 800th Military Police Brigade*. 2004.

[118] Committee on Armed Services. *Inquiry into the Treatment of Detainees in U.S. Custody*. 2008.

[119] U.S. Department of the Army. Combat and Operational Stress Control Manual for Leaders and Soldiers. *Field Manual 6-22.5*. Washington, DC 2009.

[120] *War Psychiatry*. Falls Church, VA: Office of the Surgeon General, United States Army.

[121] Hawker DM, Durkin J, Hawker DSJ. To debrief or not to debrief our heroes: that is the question. *Clinical Psychology & Psychotherapy*. 2011;18(6):453-463.

[122] Jennings B, Kahn J, Mastroianni A, Parker LS. *Ethics and public health: model curriculum*. 2003.

[123] Behnke S. What kind of issue is it? A "four-bin" approach to ethics consultation is helpful in practice settings. *Monitor on Psychology*. 2014;45(2).

[124] *Defense Health Board Medical Ethics Dual Loyalties Tasking* [PowerPoint]. Falls Church, VA 2014.

[125] Beam TE, Howe EG. A Proposed Ethic for Military Medicine. In: Sparacino LR, Pellegrino ED, eds. *Military Medical Ethics*. Vol 2. Washington, DC: Office of the Surgeon General U.S. Army, Borden Institute, Walter Reed Army Medical Center; 2003:851-865.

[126] Lehmann LS, Kasoff WS, Koch P, Federman DD. A survey of medical ethics education at U.S. and Canadian medical schools. *Acad. Med.* Jul 2004;79(7):682-689.

[127] Grady C, Danis M, Soeken KL, et al. Does ethics education influence the moral action of practicing nurses and social workers? *Am. J. Bioeth.* Apr 2008;8(4):4-11.

[128] Burkemper JE, DuBois JM, Lavin MA, Meyer GA, McSweeney M. Ethics education in MSN programs: a study of national trends. *Nurs. Educ. Perspect.* Jan-Feb 2007;28(1):10 17.

[129] World Health Organization. *Module for Teaching Medical Ethics to Undergraduates*. 2009.

[130] Uniformed Services University of the Health Sciences. *Department of Medical & Clinical Psychology Handbook: 2014-2015*. Bethesda, MD 2013.

[131] Gilliland WR. Request to the Defense Health Board to provide teaching of ethical guidelines and practices for the F. Edward Hebert School of Medicine. In: Thompson R, ed. Bethesda, MD: Uniformed Services University of the Health Sciences; 2013.

[132] Uniformed Services University of the Health Sciences. Curriculum: molecules to military medicine. 2014; http://www.usuhs.mil/curriculum/faq.html. Accessed January 30, 2015.

[133] Thompson R. USUHS Physicians % of new accessions vs % of sr medical officers. In: Rouse D, ed2015.

[134] Romano CA. Request to the Defense Health Board to provide details of teaching ethical guidelines and practices for the Daniel K. Inouye Graduate School of Nursing. In: Thompson AM, ed. Bethesda, MD: Uniformed Services University of the Health Sciences; 2014.

[135] Uniformed Services University of the Health Sciences. Information Handbook for Graduate Medical and Public Health Programs. In: The Department of Preventive Medicine and Biometrics, ed2014.

[136] Uniformed Services University of the Health Sciences. Ethics and professionalism education in the postgraduate dental school In: Board DH, ed. Bethesda, MD 2014.

[137] Uniformed Services University of the Health Sciences. *Annual Report.* Bethesda, MD: Uniformed Services University of the Health Sciences;2006.

[138] Walter Reed-Bethesda Ethics Committee and Department of Pastoral Care. Annual Healthcare Ethics Symposium June 4th and 5th 2014. 2014.

[139] Navy Medicine Professional Development Center. General Continuing Medical Education Information for Walter Reed Medical Ethics Short Course Fall 2013. 2014.

[140] Medscape. State CME requirements. 2014; http://www.medscape.org/public/state requirements. Accessed January 30, 2015.

[141] U.S. Department of Defense. About the Department of Defense (DoD). http://www.defense.gov/about/#mission. Accessed January 30, 2015.

[142] Mill JS. *Utilitarianism.* Hackett Publishing Company; 1979.

[143] Thomasma DC, Marshall PA. *Clinical medical ethics: cases and reading.* New York, NY: New York University Press; 1995.

[144] United Nations. Principles of Medical Ethics relevant to the Role of Health Personnel, particularly Physicians, in the Protection of Prisoners and Detainees against Torture and Other Cruel, Inhuman or Degrading Treatment or Punishment. Vol General Assembly resolution 37/1941982.

[145] American Medical Association. AMA Code of Medical Ethics. *Opinion 2.067 Torture* 1999.

[146] World Medical Association. WMA Declaration of Malta on Hunger Strikers. 2006.

In: U.S. Military Medical Professionals
Editor: Erin Andrews

ISBN: 978-1-63484-697-4
© 2016 Nova Science Publishers, Inc.

Chapter 2

A PROPOSED ETHIC
FOR MILITARY MEDICINE*

Thomas E. Beam and Edmund G. Howe

INTRODUCTION

Directly applying ethical principles from civilian medical ethics may not be appropriate in military medicine. The basic discrepancy between the two settings involves their goals and how these goals can be achieved. In the military, the objective is to defeat the enemy; this often involves killing enemy soldiers. When the mission of protecting society requires it, all members of the military must subordinate other value priorities to effect this end of overpowering an enemy by whatever legal and moral means necessary. For military physicians, this may involve sacrificing their patients' interests when required by the military mission of protecting society. Civilian doctors, in contrast, generally can focus on primary medical goals, such as trying to save patients' lives, or halt the spread of disease. This same discrepancy in goals underlies the core ethical quandary military physicians face, which, in one way or another, permeates this book.

That is, military physicians balance giving absolute priority to the principle of military necessity (adopting a military role-specific ethic) with

---

* This is an edited, reformatted and augmented version of text that originally appeared as Chapter 27 in Military Medical Ethics, Volume 2, issued by the Office of the Surgeon General, Borden Institute, Walter Reed Army Medical Center, 2003.

giving moral weight to their traditional civilian medical priorities. When they do the latter, they give patients' interests some moral weight even though this conflicts with interests that might further military interests. However, as we will discuss later in this chapter, there is a distinction between military necessity, which is absolute, and military interests, which are not.

Difficulty arises in ascertaining what constitutes true military necessity involving medical decisions. Making this determination is among the most difficult ethical decisions military physicians and military medical leaders face. This chapter will propose a decision-making process that could be used by policy makers and military physicians. Understanding this process can help individual physicians accept those situations in which they must place the needs of the military over those of their patients. Individual physicians can also use the process in their own practices when policy or guidance from commanders is not clearly stated.

A Proposed Military Medical Ethic

The tensions between a military doctor's duties to his patients and to the command (and society) have been discussed extensively in the previous chapters of these volumes. In this final chapter, we will offer a proposed military medical ethic and use a decision-making algorithm to suggest how physicians and policy makers might best go about balancing these competing values.

Physician First, Officer Second?

We propose as a basis for beginning discussion that a military physician is primarily a physician and in most instances makes decisions on this basis rather than as a military officer. Although this statement appears to emphasize the differences between medicine and the military, the instances of there being a significant conflict are very rare. In general, excellent medical care for soldiers—as patients—is in the best interests of the soldier, the physician, and the military. Therefore, in almost all situations, the military physician thinks and acts as a physician primarily and practices patient-centered medicine. Lieutenant General Ronald Blanck,[1] The Surgeon General of the US Army from 1996 to 2000, and others[2–4] have advanced this position. The issue of a military physician being a military officer usually does not become a factor in his decisions. Society generally expects physicians, even physicians in uniform, to place the interests of patients, including soldiers, above all other considerations. However, society also expects military members to sacrifice personal safety and comfort to "protect and defend" its interests. Therefore, there are situations in which the conflicting obligations (mixed agency) become evident. In these situations, the military physician will need to balance his duties to his patient with his obligations as a military officer or give absolute priority to military needs.

In situations of military necessity, military physicians must give absolute priority to military needs. Therefore, priority will appropriately be given to protecting and defending society when society's interests would be significantly sacrificed as a result of not doing so. The United States Code[5] allows the Secretary of the Army to direct the medical care of any individual on active duty. He may determine that the needs of the Army are so significant that they must override those of the soldier-patient. Policy makers, both medical and tactical, and medical leaders advise him on the pertinent factors to assist him in making his decision.

The original assumption—that military physicians are doctors first and officers second—may seem to be contrary to this legal authority granted to the Secretary of the Army. However it is an accurate description of the reality seen in military medicine. The concept that the soldier "belongs" to the United States government with medical care routinely being forced upon the soldier is simply not the case. Although statutory authority is in place to address relatively unusual situations in which enforced treatment is required to accomplish the military mission, the Secretary of the Army rarely mandates medical treatment. Therefore, the physician usually is able to maintain his medical identity and act as if he were a physician in a civilian setting by respecting the autonomy of his soldier-patient.

The decision to override soldiers' interests (as patients) inevitably is, and should be, agonizing and should not be exercised without significant, combat-related reasons for doing so. The best approach to balancing these social and individual soldier-patient interests is to presume that autonomy of the soldier as a patient is the primary force in medical decision making but that exceptions can be justified by overarching societal requirements related to the military's mission.

The concept of a physician acting as a doctor first and an officer second also implies that sometimes the physician voluntarily limits exercising his power because the soldier-patient is uniquely vulnerable to coercion. Exercising power may more readily become unethical coercion within military medicine than in the voluntary patient–physician relationship seen in the civilian community. Thus, this power should be more limited, as it has been in some other contexts. Miranda-like warnings were adopted in the military to protect soldiers from such inherent coercion, for example, before they were required in the civilian sector.

Limited Exercise of Power

In all medical decisions there is a significant imbalance of power within the patient–physician relationship (see Chapter 1, The Moral Foundations of the Patient–Physician Relationship: The Essence of Medical Ethics). In civilian medicine, this is recognized as one of the reasons the principle of autonomy assumes a primary role in ethical decision making. The patient is in a vulnerable position and must be protected. This same vulnerability exists within the military patient–physician relationship but it is accentuated because of unique military pressures. The military is a hierarchical organization and its operation is based on the presumption of obedience. This is required for its primary mission of protecting society. Orders must be obeyed promptly and questioned only in rare cases of almost certain illegality or immorality. Although there are procedures for refusing to obey an order,[6] circumstances that require a soldier to exercise this option are, and should be, extremely rare. However, this deference to the authority of superiors makes soldiers much more likely to be vulnerable when medical decisions regarding them are made. Further, all military physicians are officers, and primarily field grade officers (majors and above). This enhances the presumption that their advice will be followed. Because it is more difficult for military patients to choose, or change, their physician, they may feel more obligated to accept the physician's advice.

The military physician also may be more likely than his civilian colleague to become used to exercising his authority. Although civilian physicians have obvious symbols of their status and power (their "uniform" consists of the white coat and stethoscope), the military physician wears his rank visibly and his power comes not only from his knowledge and training as a physician but also from his being commissioned as an officer in the military. In military contexts, his orders, ethically as well as legally, are to be obeyed. The subtle difference between military orders and medical ones can become blurred and this could lead to an abuse of the physician's power. It is important to remember, however, that the military physician does not have legal authority to order a soldier-patient to undergo treatment. This authority is given to the soldier's commander or, in rare circumstances, the hospital commander. The soldier-patient, however, is more likely to defer to the authority of any superior officer (including medical officers) and this perception increases his vulnerability.

Another concern arises because the military physician may overidentify with his military unit. (Chapter 13, Medical Ethics on the Battlefield: The Crucible of Military Medical Ethics, addresses this in greater detail.) This can occur because of the military training and conditioning he receives, particularly if he is a member of an elite unit.[7] This over-identification with the military unit may result in his modeling his medical orders on a military model. This also can significantly increase the likelihood of an abuse of power. The military physician must be extremely aware of this possibility and be vigilant to prevent this abuse from occurring.

For these reasons, more restraint should be applied in military medical decision making than in the civilian sector. The line of restraint must be drawn clearly and, indeed, more closely for the military physician than his civilian colleague.

Compensatory Justice

Another concept that we believe merits moral weight is that of compensatory justice. This concept was introduced in Chapter 26, A Look Toward the Future, but will be amplified here. Although the military has an obligation to fulfill its mission to protect society, society has a reciprocal obligation to those who have willingly placed themselves in harm's way. One of the ways this could be accomplished is by providing soldiers, in appropriate contexts, "compensatory justice." Soldiers sacrifice much in performing their duty to society. They, of course, may die in service to their country. They also give up many of the freedoms that American citizens enjoy. These freedoms, ironically, are in many cases those that, as soldiers, they may die to preserve (see Chapter 9, The Soldier and Autonomy). This loss of freedom is necessary to preserve the "good order and discipline" in the armed forces that enables the armed forces to accomplish their mission of protecting society. Therefore, society owes a great debt of gratitude to its protectors.

Because of this debt, society should support the military's choosing to compensate its members in special ways. This is fair and appropriate. The government provides special pay for those in combat, income tax exemptions for portions of their pay, and other tangible expressions of gratitude for dangerous service. Individual members of society may choose to express their gratitude as well. During and after recent conflicts many businesses and individuals have made special benefits available to soldiers, including donating free rooms in hotels, offering special travel opportunities to resorts or tourist attractions, and deferring interest payments on purchases made by soldiers.

Military medicine has opportunities as well to compensate its beneficiaries in extra ways. Free access to medical care for soldiers and their families and free dental care for soldiers have been benefits associated with military service. Some programs, such as using DNA (deoxyribonucleic acid) analysis to identify remains of soldiers even after they have left active duty, may give special benefits as well. In evaluating new technologies and procedures (as seen in Chapter 26), policy decision makers also can choose to include promising treatments or programs that benefit soldiers and their families. This can be justified as special compensation for harms, both actual and potential, associated with military service. This is the concept of compensatory justice.

THE DECISION–MAKING PROCESS

As stated before, decisions requiring prioritizing the conflicting goals of the military and of medicine can be the most difficult military leaders and military physicians face. The following algorithms are offered not as the definitive "solution" to these dilemmas but as a means for examining the process used to arrive at the decision. As will be seen, there are uncertainties and ambiguities inherent in all decisions. This is particularly true in those involving both clinical medicine and combat. The basic decision often becomes that of determining who "gets" to make the decision and once that determination is made, what criteria are the appropriate ones for deciding. There can be a conflict in moral views—the military priority of the mission as opposed to the medical priority of the individual patient.

Military Medical Ethics Decision-Making Algorithm

Another way to further protect soldiers might be to follow loose guidelines of a decision-making algorithm to help determine appropriate use of this increased power and to help avoid its misuse. We propose a decision matrix for consideration (Figure 1). The algorithm as presented here is greatly streamlined; one should not assume that complicated decisions could necessarily be made in these few steps. However, this simplified version clarifies a process that may be optimal. Thus it can be useful to policy makers and military physicians in making optimal moral decisions. We will describe the decision-making process using the algorithm and give examples of some possible applications.

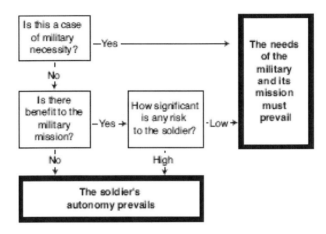

Figure 1. Military medical ethics decision making.

Decision Point #1: Assessing Military Necessity

The first decision point is that of military necessity. This concept has been discussed in previous chapters and is briefly reiterated here in this chapter. Simply stated, there are situations in which military needs are likely to be absolute. This occurs whenever the completion of the mission could be significantly affected. As discussed previously, the survival of the society is the ultimate end of the military profession. Because this goal is absolute, the needs of individuals must be considered secondary and ethically can be overridden by military necessity. Situations requiring this are not common, but they are frequent enough to cause controversy and can generate much emotion. Even if military necessity exists only in the rarest of situations, determining when it exists requires someone to make this judgment. As previously discussed, the Secretary of the Army or his designee has the statutory authority to determine if and when this military necessity exists.

In situations of military necessity, soldier autonomy can (and should) be overridden. For example, a soldier can legally be ordered to risk his life to attack an enemy's fortified position if the overall mission requires this.

Analogously, soldiers give up a certain amount of their autonomy in medical decisions as well. Similarly, physicians in the military also have their autonomy limited in certain circumstances. Physicians can be ordered to treat soldiers, even if soldiers refuse treatment, if military necessity is present. The military has this right and, due to its mission to protect society, has an affirmative obligation to do so.

Yet, if soldiers are to be placed in harm's way, a just society has an obligation to provide whatever protection it can to those soldiers. Society can expect all safe and effective protective measures to be used for its sons and daughters serving in the military. It is possible that the soldiers can't be fully informed about all the potential risks they face, but education may help soldiers anticipate when their autonomy may be overridden on the basis of military necessity. Education may also prevent some of the controversies that have occurred recently in situations in which it has been determined that overriding soldiers' autonomy is necessary.

To illustrate the strength of the justification underlying military physicians following this principle, they should adhere to it even when soldiers are subject to the draft. When military service is voluntary, persons can avoid these mandatory measures and the bodily intrusiveness they may bring about by not volunteering. If there is a draft, they have no choice. Conscription is itself justifiable on grounds that are wholly consistent with the foregoing ethical analysis. Its justification lies solely in its being necessary for the nation's survival.

Decision Point #2: Providing Benefit to the Military

If the situation is not one of military necessity, but rather one of merely providing benefit to the military, the second algorithm decision point arises. In discussing benefit to the military, it is important to distinguish that this benefit is not financial or some vague organizational benefit. Counting these gains as benefit would allow almost any decision to be interpreted as beneficial to the military. The definition of benefit intended here is instead one that truly benefits the mission the military is assigned—to protect and defend the country. Thus, the benefit is actually ultimately to society. It must be directly beneficial to the accomplishment of the mission. If this strict definition of benefit is not satisfied, the military should not override the soldier's right to make his own decision in medical interventions. This is analogous to the harm principle more fully discussed in Chapter 9, The Soldier and Autonomy. If there is true benefit to the military, using the strict definition of benefit, the next algorithm decision point, looking at the risk to the soldier, occurs.

Decision Point #3: Assessing Risk to the Soldier

In situations in which there is a true benefit to the military as defined above, the risk posed by the medical intervention to the soldier must be balanced against that benefit. This is a familiar decision matrix for all clinicians because this is the model for medical recommendations used in the daily practice of medicine. We maintain that if there is high risk to the soldier and if there is no true military necessity, but rather only benefit to the military mission, the soldier's autonomy in medical decisions should not be overridden. This may help prevent abuses of power in making these decisions. As previously discussed, because there is such a power inequality within the military, and because soldiers must of necessity give up their autonomy in many nonmedical military situations, drawing the line on the side of protecting their remaining autonomy under these circumstances is ethically not only defensible but optimal. In so doing, abuses of military physicians' and commanders' power may be decreased.

Conversely, if the benefit to the military mission is significant and the risk to the soldier is minimal, there is a stronger argument to override the soldier's autonomy. The soldier has accepted a certain limitation of his autonomy. He has accepted the mission of protecting his country, even at the risk of losing his life. Therefore, it is only consistent that he should accept some level of personal risk when the benefit to the military is substantial. In this case, we believe it is appropriate to override the soldier's autonomy for the benefit of the military mission.

We recognize that the terms "limited," "significant," "high," and "low" are not absolute. There is always a considerable level of uncertainty in these policy decisions. This also raises the other obvious issue of who has the right to assign these terms both now and in the future. Legally, as stated before, the Secretary of the Army or his designee, advised by his medical and tactical commanders, has this right.

This raises the additional issue of assigning levels of risk and benefit to decisions whose impact will only become clear in the future. As discussed in Chapter 12, Ethical Issues in Military Medicine, it may be necessary for the commander, informed by experts on his staff, to make ethical and legal decisions based on his view of the situation, because only he has the ultimate overall vision and responsibility for making the decisions that will affect the entire situation. The medical officer must participate as one of these experts, and can certainly offer a soldier-patient–centered focus, but ultimately policy decisions need to be made by the policy makers, and in the military this function resides in the chain of command. Representatives of the Judge

Advocate General will also be involved in these decisions. The previous discussion reviewed the ethical bases for decision making but the relevant laws and regulations must always be considered. In fact, they usually warrant the most moral weight in determining what physicians should do.

Applying the Military Medical Ethics Decision-Making Algorithm

We will now provide some examples and show how they can be analyzed using the military medical ethics decision-making algorithm (Figure 1).

The initial examples, which will be examined in some detail, involve policy decisions. The individual physician can use them to understand how policy decisions are made. They can also help him understand the competing loyalties he may feel in these situations and, more particularly, that though they may cause emotional pain, this does not mean they are "wrong." Other examples from individual clinical situations will be mentioned to demonstrate the application of the algorithm in the patient–physician relationship.

Policy Applications

Three areas of policy applications will be explored in this discussion: (1) acting when military necessity prevails; (2) balancing military benefit with individual risk; and (3) acting when there is minimal military benefit.

When Military Necessity Prevails. A recent context in which military physicians have had an absolute obligation to place the military's interests first is when prophylactic agents may have been needed to protect soldiers from the effects of biological and chemical weaponry. This occurred during the Persian Gulf War (1990–1991). As is discussed in Chapter 12 (Mixed Agency in Military Medicine: Ethical Roles in Conflict), it was then feared that Saddam Hussein, the leader of Iraq and its military, might use this weaponry. This fear continued until the removal of Hussein from power in 2003.

The question arose whether the use of protective agents determined to have benefit should be mandatory or voluntary. Because this weaponry could have been deadly, it was decided that although these agents had not been fully tested on humans for this battlefield purpose, their use should be mandatory.[8] Again, as discussed in Chapter 12, the justification for this was military necessity. If soldiers were not protected from chemical and biological agents, many of them would have died had the agents been used.[9] The military leaders, both combat and medical, felt that the threat that these agents may be used was credible. If inordinate numbers of soldiers died or were incapacitated because of their exposure to these agents, the battle or even the entire war could have been lost. It was necessary, therefore, to require soldiers to use these agents.

On the algorithm, the first decision point indicates that if it is militarily necessary for the accomplishment of the mission, the proposed intervention may legitimately be required. Obviously, in making this decision, the leaders must examine the expected risks and benefits of all courses of action before making a decision. Their intent is to protect the fighting force to enable it to accomplish the mission.

Subsequent events bring the ethical conflict raised by this question still more sharply into focus. Many service persons after returning from the Persian Gulf presented with symptoms that have been grouped together, designated as the Gulf War illnesses. The etiology of these symptoms remains unclear.[10,11] Nonetheless, some persons believe that the use of these protective agents and this syndrome may be related. The anger some feel highlights the reality that when military physicians override soldiers' autonomy, even on the grounds of military necessity, the long-term adverse consequences may be considerable.

More recently, since the terrorist attacks of September 11, 2001, deaths have occurred due to anthrax being sent through the federal mail system. This outcome highlights why the use of some of these protective agents may be a military necessity. One of the authors (EGH) participated in the discussion concerning the ethics of using prophylactic agents, including vaccines against biological weaponry, prior to the Persian Gulf War. The decision-making process was very similar to that just described for other agents used in the Persian Gulf War. Had Saddam Hussein used biological weaponry, many thousands of soldiers could have been killed and the war could have been lost. This risk could not be allowed. The decision in response to this threat now is to attempt to protect all service members from anthrax by vaccination.[12]

This policy has been adopted because the risk to soldiers from vaccination is minimal and the benefit to the soldier, the military, and society, is felt to be significant.[13,14]

This policy is, and should be, continually reevaluated as events and circumstances change. An organization outside the Department of Defense (DoD) may be able to examine the policy with more objectivity, or at least may be perceived as more objective. To further these ends, the Institute of Medicine, an organization clearly independent from the DoD, was invited to evaluate the safety and effectiveness of the anthrax vaccine. Although the study was funded by the military, that did not influence the committee. In fact, as Dr. Brian Strom, the chair of the committee, asserts: "If [the committee] had a bias to begin with, it probably was against the military. I felt we just had to turn over the right stone and we'd find a smoking gun out there. But we didn't find it, and we looked hard."[15] Their report, which was made public in 2002, clearly supports the conclusion that the vaccine is safe and effective. Further, it is likely to be effective against all strains of anthrax because it targets the toxin and not the cell. Independent reviews such as this can assist those establishing policy to be certain that the interventions will indeed improve the mission capability.

In civilian contexts, societies requiring persons to take such agents or to face criminal sanctions generally would be legally impermissible and ethically reprehensible. However, even in the civilian context, citizens' freedom can be curtailed to protect the greater population. This occurs, for example, when persons in a region need to be quarantined. The principle underlying military physicians' acting on the basis of necessity in military and civilian contexts is, in fact, the same.[16] Society has a right to require some degree of sacrifice from its citizens to protect the health and well-being of other members of the society. However, it is likely that a military physician will encounter this situation more frequently in his career than would a civilian physician.[17] Military physicians' obligation to respond on the basis of this necessity is absolute in principle. However, they still must exercise moral discretion when responding. When deciding whether a prophylactic agent should be used, military physicians and leaders must assess the relative benefits and burdens.[18] The point at which this ratio is sufficiently high that an agent's use should be made mandatory is, of course, an ethical decision.

All medical decisions involve ethical judgments because the benefits must be judged as worth the risk and there cannot help but be differing moral views on when this point has been reached. This is readily apparent in regard to new biological threats such as the present threat of smallpox.[19,20] Here, the benefits versus burdens are well established clinically.[21] Yet, when, and for whom, this vaccination should be reinstituted requires some persons' judgment. The question whether prophylactic agents should be used (and who should decide) becomes still more complicated when the military occupies a foreign territory. Should citizens in an occupied country be offered protection? Should prisoners of war be offered protection?[22,23] We believe it would be optimal for the protection to be offered, but we realize there may be inadequate supplies. Once again, the ethical judgment involves prioritizing the needs of potential patients with other needs of society.

Likewise, new biological or chemical weapons may be developed by hostile nations. If they are developed, efforts must and will be undertaken to find prophylactic agents quickly.[24,25] Whether such agents, just developed, should be used to protect soldiers, despite their being new, is an ethical judgment involving their relative benefits versus burdens. An ethical question that also always will be present when supplies are limited is whose needs should be prioritized. This is currently being debated in regard to available supplies of anthrax vaccine. To be consistent with the principle of military necessity, the vaccine first should be given to all those most needed to win the war. Only thereafter should the recipient pool be expanded. Who should be included in this first group and how far its margins should reach requires, of course, an ethical judgment.

It is critically important for military physicians to be aware of this inconsistency (between having to adopt a military role-specific ethic due to military necessity on one hand, but still having to exercise moral judgment in implementing this ethic on the other) when they apply the algorithm introduced above. When adopting a military role-specific ethic, they must know that though in principle their obligation is absolute, in implementing this principle they will never be able to avoid applying ethical discretion. Therefore, when military physicians seek to use the algorithm we have proposed, they should feel wholly justified in acting inflexibly and according to their role-specific military ethic if and when this is required by military necessity. However, they should feel justified to do this if, and only if, this is militarily required. They should remain aware, however, that notwithstanding their total justification in making this choice, there are many ethical judgments they cannot avoid in its implementation.

Military Benefit Balanced With Individual Risk. An example demonstrating attempts to balance the benefits to the military against the risks to the individual is that of epidemiologic studies of human immunodeficiency virus (HIV) and acquired immunodeficiency syndrome (AIDS) when the disease was first identified. Because homosexual contact was a factor in the spread of the infection, it was important to assess its prevalence. Yet, homosexuality was, and remains, a ground for discharge from the military.[26] If HIV positive soldiers admitted that they were homosexual during questioning about their risk factors, under normal circumstances they would have risked being involuntarily separated from the military. The military, on the other hand, obtained benefit from ascertaining the true etiology of HIV infection. In this instance, the benefit to the military, as well as the risk to the soldier from being identified as homosexual, is clear. Several policy decisions were made over time to attempt to resolve this issue.

In 1985, Casper Weinberger, then the Secretary of Defense, made the decision to allow confidentiality for soldiers who acknowledged their homosexuality during epidemiological studies, but not if their homosexuality was discovered under other circumstances.[27] Congress expanded this protection through legislation in 1986 by precluding not only involuntary separation, but also other adverse actions that could negatively influence the soldier's career.[28] This decision regarded the benefit the military obtained from accurate data concerning the etiology of HIV infection as being so significant that special legal provisions were enacted to attempt to minimize the real risk of harm to soldiers. It placed less weight on benefits accrued to the military from identifying and separating homosexual soldiers as long as they were not identifiable by other means (ie, as long as they were discreet).

On the other hand, the protection did not extend to security clearances. If soldiers were found to be homosexual, even through epidemiological assessment, their security clearances could be denied or revoked.[29,30] The apparent rationale for this decision seems to be the assessment that homosexual soldiers did represent a higher likelihood of being compromised because of their sexual preferences than did heterosexual soldiers. The military perceived the benefit from preventing a breach of security as outweighing the risk of harm to the soldier.

Although this assessment of the factors involved in this particular decision may not be the only interpretation possible, it serves as a good example of policy makers balancing risks and benefits in making their decisions. Furthermore, it demonstrates the model of civilian oversight of the military that exists in the United States.

Minimal Military Benefit. A final policy issue that will be analyzed using the decision-making algorithm is that of the DNA repository. Using DNA technology, the military has been able to identify remains of soldiers from previous battles, including the remains of Air Force First Lieutenant Michael Blassie as the Unknown Soldier of the Vietnam War.[31] The technique involves the use of DNA taken from the remains of an unidentified soldier and comparing it with DNA taken from living family members of missing soldiers. It is far superior to using other forms of identification, including fingerprints, scars and blemishes, or dental records. The DNA used in this technique is found in the mitochondria of all cells and is passed within the ovum of the mother to her children.[32] If there are consistent similarities on the mitochondrial DNA patterns, the military may be able to identify the previously unidentified remains of a soldier. Obviously this requires some element of chance and luck, in that there are many soldiers missing in action and, although circumstances can narrow the potential matches somewhat, there is still a large pool of potential matches. It is also possible that the mother and siblings of the soldier may not be available to donate cells for DNA testing.

This uncertainty and, to some degree, the amount of DNA to be examined for similarity can be overcome by having actual DNA from the soldier. In 1992, the Department of Defense established a repository of DNA samples to be used for this purpose with samples of blood and other cells.[33] All members of the military, active duty and reserve, were required to supply these samples.

The possible benefit for families is a compelling argument in favor of offering this to soldiers. They can be spared the horror of wondering if their loved one is suffering in a prisoner of war camp somewhere. Families can then proceed through the grieving process as well as finalizing legal and financial documents.

The ability to identify remains is not, however, militarily necessary for the mission to succeed. However, it may be beneficial to the military to be able to identify its dead and to change the status of the soldier from missing to deceased. Other soldiers may benefit as well from knowing that remains can be promptly and accurately identified. It would also be beneficial to the soldier to know that his family would be spared the uncertainty of not knowing if he were dead or a prisoner of war. The military services have established the goal of never having an unidentified soldier in future conflicts.

The next question in the algorithm involves risk to the individual. There is a risk that the DNA could be used in ways that would harm the person, such as potential invasion of privacy. DNA carries unique information and this information can be used not only for remains identification, but also for prediction of genetic diseases. For example, genetic profiling for career advancement or medical insurance are possible harms that could come from the misuse of this information. However, the DNA repository does not analyze the DNA for genetic diseases because the samples would be used only for comparison with DNA taken from the unidentified remains of a US service member.[34]

In 1996, the Department of Defense issued a policy clarifying four possible uses of the DNA as (1) identification of human remains, (2) internal quality assurance activities, (3) other activities for which the donor or surviving next of kin specifically consents, and (4) court-ordered examination for prosecution of serious crimes and only after review by the Department of Defense General Counsel.[35-37] Although safeguards have been established to help prevent potential harms, there are still concerns about them as evidenced by several service members refusing to have their DNA taken and stored. Some of these were even tried by court martial and found guilty of refusing a lawful order.[38]

Depending on the determination of the risk to the soldier, it would be possible to decide to require soldiers to submit the DNA samples, or to decide to make participation in the DNA remains identification program voluntary depending on the weighting of conflicting values. Of course, if there is no true benefit to the military mission, the soldier's autonomy should not be overridden.

In summary, these three areas of policy application—(1) when military necessity prevails, (2) military benefit balanced with individual risk, and (3) minimal military benefit—represent the continuum along which these different decisions can be made.

Clinical Examples

The algorithm can also be applied in the clinical setting. Chapter 12 demonstrates this with the discussions of situations that require adopting a military role-specific ethic, situations in which discretion should be applied, and situations in which a medical role-specific ethic possibly should be adopted. An example of using the algorithm in a clinical situation requiring a military role-specific ethic because military necessity is absolute is that of treating combat stress disorder. In Chapter 12, Howe states that a floodgate phenomenon could occur if combat stress disorder is treated by evacuation from the theater. This could significantly affect the military's being able to accomplish its mission. To avoid this likelihood, soldiers with combat stress disorder must be returned to duty, even if this violates their wishes.

The example of the alcoholic general (in Case Study 12-1), in which the wife revealed to her physician that her husband (a commanding general) was an alcoholic, is an example demonstrating a high risk to the patient (the wife in this example— her marriage and her relationship with the physician) and the expected low level of benefit to the military (by having the general's addiction identified). The risk in this case was judged to be greater than the benefit to the military. If the general were impaired significantly, or if his level of responsibility were great enough, the opposite decision could possibly have been made based on a higher level of benefit to the military and this level approaching military necessity.

A possible example of there being essentially no benefit to the military is that of the affair (discussed in Case Study 12-4) in which the physician wanted to report his patient after the patient admitted to an adulterous relationship. The physician's colleagues were convinced that there was a negligible benefit to the military in exposing the affair and that, if there were no benefit, it should not be reported.

These clinical examples demonstrate the varying application of the algorithm, based on the physician assigning values to the competing goals. This is a familiar model to all clinicians, in that assessing risk/benefit ratios is a basis for all clinical decision making. Applying a similar model to ethical decision making is a reasonable extension of a basic clinical skill.

Conflicts Between Ethics and the Law: An Algorithm

Another difficult dilemma arises when law and ethics appear to be in conflict. A discussion of the legal basis of military medicine was presented in detail in Chapter 12, Mixed Agency in Military Medicine: Ethical Roles in Conflict. The military physician must also have some knowledge of military law and of the law of warfare (as discussed in Chapter 8, Just War Doctrine and the International Law of War), as well as of those laws applying specifically to medicine (as discussed in Chapter 23, Military Medicine in War: The Geneva Conventions Today). If a military physician has doubts about the legal requirements of military medicine, he should consult with others who have more experience with these issues, whether they are members of the Judge Advocate General Corps or more senior military physicians who have dealt with such matters in the past. It is essential that individual physicians understand the legally imposed limits on their autonomy required by the military mission when exercising discretion to avoid suboptimal outcomes for their soldier-patients, themselves, and the military overall. In some instances, for example, the law should warrant great weight; in others, legal requirements may be absent and thus warrant little, if any, weight.

At the same time, the physician needs to be aware that decisions made using ethical analysis may not be the same as those made using legal analysis.

When the two differ, the most difficult questions regarding discretion may arise. This conflict will be explored using another algorithm (Figure 2). The process involved is similar to that available to all soldiers if they are concerned about the legality of an order; therefore commanders are familiar with this concept. As already stated, these issues are extremely complex. Thus, although the algorithm given may help frame the discussion and provide some basis for identifying underlying assumptions and initially proceeding, no simplified decision matrix can "solve" ethical dilemmas.

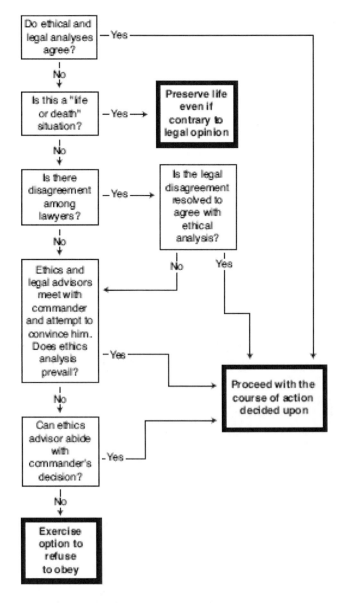

Figure 2. Conflicts between ethics and the law.

A Proposed Ethic for Military Medicine 127

Generally a legal analysis generates the same conclusion as ethical analysis. Malpractice lawyers thus say rightly that the best protection from lawsuits is to practice good medicine. Practicing good clinical medicine is practicing not only legally good medicine, but ethically good medicine as well. However, the law provides only a "good" minimum level of practice (what one must do or must not do to prevent lawsuits), whereas ethics provides a higher level of practice (what one ought to do). Practicing good ethical medicine would thus not only satisfy the legal requirements but also meet a higher standard of patient care.

There is significant moral weight due the law. Legal traditions have been developed through a rigorous series of examinations, cross-examinations, challenges, and astute judgments. Moreover, the law warrants respect even when it conflicts with ethics because it represents the best practice for deciding policy when persons dissent. Society therefore rightly expects the military, and military physicians, to operate within the constraints of the law. However, there are occasions in which the decision suggested by the legal advisors may differ from that determined by ethical analysis. This occurs in civilian medicine as well and can cause discomfort in ethics committees and ethics consultants. In ethics consultations, it is important for legal interpretations to be subject to challenge and discussion. The lawyer's interpretation should not automatically shut down all further discussion.

Furthermore, lawyers can (and often do) disagree on specific interpretations of the law, so an individual lawyer's interpretation of the law may not reflect the only way the law can be applied. It also may not be the only law applicable or the most appropriate law for the situation. And in many cases the law does not yet exist. Statutes dealing with an ethically conflicted situation sometimes have not yet been enacted and precedent cases may have not yet been adjudicated. When one of the courses of action would lead to the death of the patient, it is appropriate to continue with actions that preserve the patient's life until all issues are resolved. This last point is best illustrated by a case.

Case Study 27-1 The Inappropriate Surrogate. An elderly man with chronic obstructive pulmonary disease was admitted to a hospital in another state for increasing respiratory distress. While in that hospital, and while he had decision-making capacity, he crafted a durable power of attorney document, naming his fiancé as the person he appointed to make decisions for him, should he be unable to do so. His clinical condition continued to worsen and he was transferred to a military tertiary medical center. While at the military medical center, he verbally informed the attending physician that he wanted his fiancé to participate in medical decision making. He continued to deteriorate and was transferred to the Intensive Care Unit and was placed on the ventilator after indicating to the physician and his fiancé that he wanted a trial of maximum medical therapy. He became incapable of participating in decision making. His wife (their divorce was completed except for the judge's ruling, which was expected within a week) arrived and ordered the ventilator discontinued. The fiancé stated that he was still early enough in the trial period that he would not want the ventilator removed. The hospital attorney advised that the durable power of attorney was only a general one and did not grant medical decision making to the fiancé, and that the spouse was the legally recognized surrogate even though they were estranged and almost divorced. Until the divorce became final, the spouse had decision-making authority.

Comment: This case demonstrates a conflict between the hospital attorney's view and the unanimous opinion of the ethics consultants, as well as the healthcare team. If the expressed wishes of the spouse were to be followed (which was advised by the attorney) this would likely lead to the patient's death. In this case the decision was made to appeal the attorney's decision and to continue medical treatment until the ethical and legal issues could be resolved.

For the military physician, this conflict can be extremely difficult, but it should not be impossible to resolve. The lawyer is the legal advisor to the commander and the ethics consultant advises on ethics. In situations of disagreement, the commander needs good advice from each; he ultimately will make the decision. In the military today, the surgeon general of each service has an ethics consultant to help him as he makes decisions that have ethical implications. Local commanders (and individual military physicians) can ask this consultant or a local ethics committee for assistance when making these decisions. Once the commander makes his decision, the physician is still, however, a moral agent and must choose how to act in light of these recommendations. If the physician is morally opposed to the commander's decision, he should inform his commander about his moral dilemma and discuss alternatives. If the situation cannot be resolved, he could request to be relieved from the situation, he could resign from the military, or he could disobey and suffer the consequences of this decision. The physician can also request a review and ruling from a higher level in the chain of command. These actions must be carefully considered but it will not usually be necessary to proceed to this point. Still, military physicians must be willing to act independently of the law if and when this seems ethically necessary. In emergency situations it may be optimal, for example, to err on the side of preserving a patient's life by not making a decision that is likely to shorten a patient's life when delaying is necessary to allow a more considered decision. This was exemplified in the case just given.

Another, more obvious, example occurred in Germany during World War II. Laws that were enacted were clearly immoral, and could have been disobeyed. Disobeying them would have consequences, possibly severe ones, but physicians could have accepted this in order to obey their consciences. As we have seen in earlier chapters, acting in conscience has risks, but this is required for persons of moral character. It will also raise moral standards in an organization.[39] Conversely, physicians who went along with Nazi policies were tried and convicted of crimes against humanity. Attempts to defend their actions by claiming that they were just following orders were unsuccessful. Particularly in a democratic society such as the United States, acting in conscience by challenging immoral laws is more likely to change the laws.

CONCLUSION

This final chapter reemphasizes the tension underlying mixed agency, or conflicting loyalty, issues. Some aspects of these are unique in the military. There are extraordinary potential differences between the realities military and civilian physicians face. Nonetheless, the ethical priorities both would adhere to under the same extreme circumstances are the same. The examples of military necessity and civilian quarantine for infectious disease are illustrative. Both give highest priority to saving the greatest number of lives. In these situations the conflict is between two goals (protecting an individual patient's interests and saving many lives), each of which is generally considered morally weighty. However, the military physician is likely to face these issues more frequently than his civilian colleague.

Civilian physicians have faced mixed agency issues as well. Physicians in sports medicine, penal institutions, and other situations in which they are employed by an organization experience conflicting loyalties similar to their military colleagues. The goals here conflicting with the patient's best interests, however, are not as clearly warranting of moral weight in all of these cases. Mixed agency issues are, however, becoming increasingly obvious in medical practice today as managed care models become prevalent. In some systems, there are pressures to avoid tests or procedures because they are expensive, even when they may be beneficial to the patient.

Several chapters in these volumes have attempted to provide some assistance to military physicians when they are faced with seemingly irreconcilable conflicts. The example in Chapter 12 of the submarine crew member who had to close the hatch on his fellow sailor in order to save the rest of the crew is illustrative. The sailor continued to have sorrow many years later over his comrade's death, but he did not feel guilt over his decision to close the hatch. This situation is analogous to a military physician's having to place priority for true military necessity over the needs of his patient. Once again, however, the conflict exists between two goals (service to the military mission of protecting society and service to the individual patient or sailor), both of which warrant moral weight.

As has been emphasized in this chapter, the military physician is a physician first and usually can continue to place his patient's interests first. It is the uncommon situation that requires placing priority on military necessity. However, as has been seen, these situations can and do arise. If military and civilian policy makers and military physicians providing care have been able to examine these issues as discussed in these volumes, and are able to apply these analyses to specific dilemmas, they may be more able to make very difficult decisions and justifiably be more able to live with them. The physician who serves in the military is in the best position to study the dilemmas and, by having examined them prior to being in an emergency situation (for example, in combat), is best able to attempt to resolve them appropriately. We hope this chapter, as well as all of the chapters in these two volumes, will generate further analysis and can help military physicians accomplish their mission in the most ethical manner possible.

REFERENCES

Blanck RR. Anthrax vaccination is based on medical evidence. *Am J Public Health.* 2000;90(8): 1326–1327.

Carter BS. Ethical concerns for physicians deployed to Operation Desert Storm. *Mil Med.* 1994; 159(1):55–59.

Cieslak TJ, Rowe JR, Kortepeter MG, et al. A field-expedient algorithmic approach to the clinical management of chemical and biological casualties. *Mil Med.* 2000;165(9): 659–662.

DNA Samples. Available at: http://www.uscg.mil/hq/mcpocg/1medical/rcdna01.htm. Accessed 1 March 2002.

Ferrari R, Russell AS. The problem of Gulf War syndrome. *Med Hypotheses.* 2001; 56(6): 697–701.

Haim M, Gdalevich M, Mimouni D, Ashkenazi I, Shemer J. Adverse reactions to smallpox vaccine: The Israeli Defence Force experience, 1991 to 1996. A comparison with previous surveys. *Mil Med.* 2000; 165(4):287–289.

Haritos-Fatouros M. The official torturer: A learning model for obedience to the authority of violence. *J Appl Soc Psychol.* 1998;18(13): 1107–1120.

Henderson DA, Inglesby TV, Bartlett JG, et al. Smallpox as a biological weapon: Medical and public health management. Working Group on Civilian Biodefense. *JAMA.* 1999;281(22): 2127–2137.

Holland MM, et al. Mitochondrial DNA sequence analysis of human skeletal remains: Identification of remains from the Vietnam War. *J Forensic Sci.* 1993;38(3): 542–553.

Howe EG, Martin E. The use of investigational drugs without obtaining servicepersons' consent in the Persian Gulf. *Hastings Cent Rep.* 1991;21: 21–24.

Howe EG. Ethical aspects of military physicians treating patients with HIV/Part one: The duty to warn. *Mil Med.* 1988; 153:7–11.

Howe EG. Ethical issues regarding mixed agency of military physicians. *Soc Sci Med.* 1986;23: 803–813.

Howe EG. Medical ethics: Are they different for the military physician? *Mil Med.* 1981;146: 837–841.

Howe EG. The Gulf War syndrome and the military medic: Whose agent is the physician? In: Zeman A, Emanuel LL, eds. *Ethical Dilemmas in Neurology.* London: WB Saunders Co; 2000: 139–156.

Jeffer EK. Command of military medical units: Grounding the paradigm. *Mil Med.* 1996;161:346–348.

Jeffer EK. Medical units: Who should command? *Mil Med.* 1990;155:413–417.

Lieutenant General Ronald R. Blanck (Retired), formerly The Surgeon General, US Army. Personal Communication, May 2002.

Longmire AW, Deshmukh N. The medical care of Iraqi enemy prisoners of war. *Mil Med.* 1991;156(12): 645–648.

Marino MT. Use of surrogate markers for drugs of military importance. *Mil Med.* 1998;163(11): 743–746.

Mayers DL. Exotic virus infections of military significance: Hemorrhagic fever viruses and pox virus infections. *Dermatol Clin.* 1999; 17(1):29–40.

Mayfield v Dalton, 901 F. Supp 300, 303 (D. Hawaii 1995).

Maze R. Hill, services debate [adverse actions] after confidential interviews. *Navy Times.* 29 June 1987: 3.

McDonald R, Cao T, Borschel R. Multiplexing for the detection of multiple biowarfare agents shows promise in the field. *Mil Med.* 2001;166(3): 237–239.

Meyer JM, Bill BJ. *Operational Law Handbook.* Charlottesville, Va: International and Operational Law Department, The Judge Advocate General's School; 2002.

Moore WL Jr, DeDonato DM, Frisina ME. *An Ethical Basis for Military Medicine.* A working draft of a paper proposal. January 1995.

Nass M. Anthrax vaccine: Model of a response to the biologic warfare threat. *Infect Dis Clin North Am.* 1999;13(1): 187–208.

National Defense Authorization Act for Fiscal Year 1987. Pub L 99-661, Division A, Title 7, 705c(1986). Codified in 10 USC 1074.

National Museum of Health and Medicine. Exhibits. Available at: http://www.natmedmuse.afip.org/exhibits/dna/identification/identification.html. Accessed 23 May 2002.

Policy concerning homosexuality in the armed forces. General Military Law, Armed Forces, 10 USC Sect 654 (2000).

Repository History. Available at: http://www.afip.org/Departments/oafme/dna/history.htm. Accessed 23 May 2002.

Request for Specimen Destruction. Available at: http://www.afip.org/Departments/oafme/dna/ EarlyDest.htm. Accessed 1 March 2002.

Strom B. As cited in: Larkin M. Anthrax vaccine is safe and effective—but needs some improvement, says IOM. *Lancet.* 2002; 359:951.

Surveillance for adverse events associated with anthrax vaccination: US Department of Defense, 1998–2000. *MMWR Morb Mortal Wkly Rep.* 2000;49(16):341–345.

The Secretary of Defense. *Policy on Identification, Surveillance and Disposition of Military Personnel Affected With HTLV-III.* Memorandum, 24 October 1985.

United States Code, Title 10. Armed Forces, Subtitle B. Army, Part II. Personnel Chapter 355. Hospitalization, Section. 3723. Approved 13 November 1998.

US Department of Defense. *Armed Forces Institute of Pathology (AFIP).* Washington, DC: DoD; 28 October 1996. DoD Directive 5124.24.

US Department of Defense. *Policy for Implementing Instructions for Early Destruction of Individual Remains Identification Reference Specimen Samples.* DoD Policy Memorandum, 4 November 1996.

Wakin MM. Wanted: Moral virtues in the military. *Hastings Cent Rep.* 1985;15(5): 25–26.

Wiener SL. Strategies for the prevention of a successful biological warfare aerosol attack. *Mil Med.* 1996; 161(5):251–256.

INDEX

#

20th century, 28

A

abuse, 17, 24, 47, 59, 69, 79, 112, 113
access, 12, 13, 17, 40, 41, 45, 48, 61, 70, 114
accessibility, 61
accessions, 78, 107
accountability, 47, 50, 67
accounting, 10, 23
acid, 98
acquired immunodeficiency syndrome (AIDS), 121
administrators, 43
advancement, 123
adverse event, 132
Afghanistan, 62, 81, 106
Africa, 81
age, 36
agencies, 49, 55, 67, 106
Air Force, 46, 47, 55, 67, 78, 92, 98, 104, 106, 122
algorithm, 75, 110, 114, 116, 118, 119, 121, 122, 123, 124, 125
American Psychiatric Association, 34, 38, 102, 103
American Psychological Association (APA), 34, 35, 38, 75, 92, 102, 103

anger, 119
anthrax, 119, 121, 132
appointments, 59
Aristotle, 94
armed conflict, 28, 36, 99, 101
armed forces, 113, 132
arthritis, 31
articulation, 47
assault, 13, 55
assessment, 55, 71, 122
assets, 16, 52, 54, 64, 67
atrocities, 29
attitudes, 50
authorit(ies), 3, 8, 25, 39, 48, 54, 55, 87, 96, 97, 111, 112, 128, 131
autonomy, 10, 24, 30, 31, 33, 34, 35, 39, 48, 69, 96, 97, 111, 112, 115, 116, 117, 119, 124, 125
awareness, 79

B

barriers, 23
base, 7, 86
basic research, 29
beneficiaries, vii, 3, 14, 61, 62, 114
benefits, 30, 31, 32, 42, 49, 74, 114, 116, 119, 120, 121, 122
bias, 120
bioethics, 12, 29, 45
black hole, 106

blood, 54, 123
breakdown, 13, 48
businesses, 114

C

care model, 129
case studies, 19, 21, 22, 72, 76, 80, 83, 84
causality, 79
CDC, 49, 98
certification, 42, 51, 95
chain of command, 3, 4, 8, 11, 12, 17, 24, 25, 43, 45, 58, 59, 60, 69, 87, 117, 128
challenges, 3, 4, 5, 11, 14, 16, 20, 21, 29, 32, 42, 43, 45, 46, 62, 67, 68, 80, 81, 82, 83, 84, 88, 127
chemical, 49, 118, 121, 130
children, 27, 67, 122
chronic obstructive pulmonary disease, 127
citizens, vii, 3, 62, 113, 120
citizenship, 47, 50
clarity, 14, 63, 64, 75
cloning, 29
Code of Federal Regulations (CFR), 30, 39, 49, 50, 58, 98, 103, 104
codes of conduct, 11, 17, 40, 43, 47, 70, 76
coercion, 31, 38, 97, 111
cognitive impairment, 96
collaboration, 29, 35
color, 35
communication, 17, 20, 21, 41, 55, 63, 69, 82, 83
communit(ies), 17, 28, 34, 38, 53, 69, 72, 85, 94, 112
compassion, 24, 34
compensation, 114
complexity, 15, 26, 66, 99
compliance, 12, 45, 49, 56
composition, 12, 44, 45
conditioning, 113
confidentiality, 15, 24, 33, 34, 36, 42, 51, 55, 56, 64, 97, 98, 122
conflict, 4, 8, 13, 15, 17, 24, 26, 31, 32, 35, 39, 41, 48, 64, 66, 70, 77, 84, 87, 96, 97, 101, 110, 114, 119, 125, 128, 129, 130

Congress, 103, 122
consensus, 10, 31, 33, 47, 81, 89
consent, 26, 29, 30, 39, 49, 58, 97, 131
Constitution, 23, 47
contingency, 52, 79
controversial, 28, 30
controversies, 41, 116
convention, 60
corruption, 29, 67, 106
cost, 65, 82
counsel, 47
covering, 21, 80, 84
crimes, 34, 123, 129
Cuba, 58, 105
cultural beliefs, 16, 68
cultural differences, 16, 53, 67, 68
culture, 9, 13, 17, 24, 27, 28, 46, 47, 48, 70, 84, 85
currency, 22, 84
curricula, 21, 76, 83
curriculum, 20, 74, 75, 77, 78, 80, 106, 107

D

danger, 14, 63
deaths, 119
decision makers, 114
decision-making process, 110, 115, 119
dental care, 114
deoxyribonucleic acid (DNA), 98, 114, 122, 123, 124, 130, 131
Department of Defense, 2, 5, 27, 30, 49, 50, 57, 58, 59, 80, 84, 88, 91, 98, 103, 104, 105, 107, 119, 123, 132
Department of Health and Human Services, 37, 104, 105
deployments, 17, 18, 20, 21, 37, 69, 71, 72, 82, 83
depression, 63
depth, 46
detainees, vii, 3, 10, 16, 21, 37, 38, 57, 58, 59, 62, 68, 83, 95, 96, 97, 103, 105
detection, 132
detention, 57, 58, 59, 96
developing nations, 67

dignity, 34, 60, 74
directives, 12, 44, 45
disability, 36
disaster, 5, 13, 15, 16, 26, 54, 67, 68, 75, 98, 99
disaster relief, 13, 15, 16, 54, 67, 68, 98, 99
disclosure, 15, 50, 55, 56, 57, 63, 64, 97
discomfort, 127
discrimination, 35, 36
diseases, 33, 54, 123
disorder, 124
disposition, 54
dissonance, 32
distress, 25, 31, 80, 101, 127
distributive justice, 32
DNA testing, 123
doctors, 103, 109, 111
draft, 91, 92, 93, 116, 132
drawing, 73, 81, 117
drugs, 24, 29, 49, 104, 131

E

education, vii, 2, 3, 5, 6, 7, 9, 16, 17, 18, 19, 20, 21, 22, 27, 29, 43, 46, 56, 61, 68, 70, 73, 74, 75, 76, 79, 80, 82, 83, 86, 89, 106, 107, 116
emergency, 24, 39, 40, 65, 95, 128, 130
emotion, 115
emotional experience, 18, 71, 72
empathy, 18, 71
employees, 50
employers, 24, 72
employment, 17, 50, 51, 69
enemies, 23, 51
enemy combatants, vii, 3, 32, 52, 62, 77
enforcement, 50
engineering, 10, 23
environment(s), vii, 2, 3, 5, 6, 9, 10, 13, 14, 16, 19, 20, 22, 25, 26, 27, 30, 33, 35, 37, 40, 42, 48, 49, 51, 54, 61, 62, 65, 66, 67, 68, 72, 78, 82, 84, 85, 86, 101, 105
epidemic, 81, 106
epidemiologic, 121
epidemiologic studies, 121

equal opportunity, 47
equality, 61
equipment, 61
erosion, 39
ethical implications, 78, 128
ethical issues, 9, 16, 21, 22, 27, 29, 41, 42, 43, 68, 73, 74, 76, 78, 79, 80, 81, 83, 84, 85
ethical standards, 3, 9, 23, 24, 25, 27, 28, 39, 50, 84
ethics, vii, 2, 5, 6, 7, 8, 9, 10, 11, 12, 13, 17, 19, 20, 21, 22, 24, 27, 28, 29, 30, 31, 32, 33, 35, 36, 40, 41, 42, 43, 44, 45, 46, 47, 48, 49, 50, 69, 70, 72, 73, 74, 75, 76, 77, 78, 79, 80, 81, 82, 83, 84, 85, 86, 87, 89, 92, 93, 95, 97, 99, 101, 102, 103, 104, 106, 107, 109, 115, 118, 119, 125, 126, 127, 128, 131
etiology, 119, 121, 122
evacuation, 51, 52, 64, 124
evidence, 130
evolution, 46
examinations, 127
execution, 32, 55, 56, 60, 63, 79
Executive Order, 47, 50, 105
exercise(s), 9, 14, 24, 27, 48, 62, 77, 78, 85, 94, 97, 112, 120, 121
expertise, 12, 43, 45, 76
exposure, 33, 66, 77, 119
external influences, 31

F

fairness, 50
faith, 23, 80
families, 41, 42, 43, 114, 123
family members, 61, 122
fasting, 96, 97
FDR, 54, 98
fear, 118
feelings, 74
fever, 131
fidelity, 34
financial, 10, 33, 50, 116, 123
fingerprints, 122

fitness, 56, 63, 95
flex, 53
flexibility, 51
flight, 77
food, 54, 96
Food and Drug Administration (FDA), 48, 49, 98, 104
force, 26, 38, 39, 48, 53, 54, 60, 62, 64, 65, 67, 97, 111, 119
foreign language, 55
formal education, 19, 73, 79
fraud, 47, 79
freedom, 35, 74, 113, 120

G

gastrointestinal bleeding, 31
gender identity, 35
genetic disease, 123
genetics, 77
Geneva Convention, 13, 51, 59, 60, 61, 65, 79, 80, 105, 125
Germany, 129
God, 23
grants, 51, 60
grotesque, 32
grounding, 47
Guantanamo, 38, 39, 58, 69, 101, 103, 105, 106
guidance, 6, 7, 11, 12, 13, 15, 17, 19, 22, 35, 37, 44, 45, 47, 49, 50, 51, 52, 54, 55, 56, 61, 63, 64, 66, 67, 69, 70, 73, 75, 86, 94, 110
guidelines, vii, 2, 4, 5, 10, 24, 30, 33, 34, 35, 37, 41, 46, 49, 53, 68, 88, 89, 96, 107, 114
guilt, 32, 130
guilty, 124

H

happiness, 50
Hawaii, 131
health, vii, 2, 3, 4, 5, 6, 7, 8, 9, 10, 11, 12, 13, 14, 15, 16, 17, 18, 19, 20, 21, 22, 23, 24, 25, 26, 27, 28, 29, 30, 31, 32, 33, 34, 35, 36, 37, 39, 40, 41, 42, 43, 44, 45, 46, 48, 49, 51, 53, 54, 55, 56, 57, 58, 59, 61, 62, 63, 64, 65, 66, 67, 68, 69, 70, 71, 72, 73, 75, 76, 78, 79, 80, 81, 82, 83, 84, 85, 86, 87, 88, 91, 94, 95, 96, 97, 99, 101, 103, 104, 120
Health and Human Services, 49
health care, vii, 2, 3, 4, 5, 6, 7, 8, 9, 10, 11, 12, 13, 14, 15, 16, 17, 18, 19, 20, 21, 22, 24, 25, 26, 27, 28, 29, 30, 31, 32, 33, 35, 36, 37, 40, 41, 42, 43, 44, 45, 46, 48, 49, 51, 53, 54, 55, 56, 57, 58, 59, 61, 62, 63, 64, 65, 66, 67, 68, 69, 70, 71, 72, 73, 75, 76, 78, 79, 80, 81, 82, 83, 84, 85, 86, 87, 88, 91, 94, 101, 103, 104
health care professionals, vii, 2, 3, 4, 5, 6, 7, 8, 9, 10, 11, 12, 13, 14, 15, 16, 17, 18, 19, 20, 21, 22, 24, 25, 26, 27, 28, 30, 31, 32, 40, 42, 43, 44, 45, 46, 49, 51, 55, 56, 58, 59, 61, 62, 63, 64, 65, 67, 68, 69, 70, 71, 72, 73, 79, 80, 81, 82, 83, 84, 85, 86, 87, 88, 91
health care programs, 104
health care sector, 14, 62
health information, 13, 15, 36, 37, 55, 56, 63, 64, 104
health services, vii, 3, 61
health status, 14, 16, 62, 63, 64, 69
history, 9, 27, 46, 47, 84, 104, 132
homosexuality, 121, 122, 132
honesty, 50, 77
host, 16, 51, 53, 54, 55, 67, 68, 77
hotels, 114
House, 106
HTLV, 132
human, 23, 29, 30, 32, 34, 35, 37, 40, 54, 74, 75, 76, 101, 106, 121, 123, 131
human health, 23
human immunodeficiency virus (HIV), 121, 122, 131
human remains, 123
human resources, 40

human right(s), 35, 75, 101, 106
human subjects, 29, 30
humanitarian aid, 26
husband, 124
Hussein, Saddam, 118, 119

isolation, 18, 20, 71, 72, 82
issues, vii, 5, 7, 16, 17, 19, 29, 39, 41, 42, 43, 45, 51, 57, 59, 62, 64, 68, 69, 72, 73, 75, 76, 81, 85, 86, 101, 125, 127, 129, 130, 131

I

ideal(s), 10, 47
identification, 113, 122, 123, 124, 132
identity, 39, 53, 111
imagination, 74
imitation, 94
immigration, 96
imprisonment, 95
improvements, 55
income, 113
income tax, 113
independence, 15, 34, 64, 97
individuals, 5, 17, 19, 20, 23, 26, 30, 31, 32, 36, 37, 39, 40, 42, 56, 61, 63, 66, 69, 70, 71, 73, 74, 81, 94, 96, 97, 98, 114, 115
inefficiency, 39
infection, 67, 121, 122
infertility, 28
influenza, 48
information sharing, 97
informed consent, 29, 30, 31, 49
infrastructure, 6, 9, 23, 27, 53, 54, 55, 72, 81, 85
injur(ies), 4, 6, 8, 15, 17, 18, 19, 25, 32, 51, 53, 63, 66, 67, 69, 71, 72, 86, 102
inmates, 39
inspections, 12, 45
institutions, 2, 5, 12, 14, 41, 45, 54, 62, 67, 76, 89, 129
integration, 75, 77
integrity, 13, 24, 35, 42, 46, 47, 48, 50, 69, 77
intelligence, 60
intelligence gathering, 60
interrogations, 26, 32, 38, 60, 103
intervention, 53, 58, 102, 117, 119
invasion of privacy, 123
Iraq, 26, 62, 118

J

jurisdiction, 50, 66
just society, 116
justification, 116, 118, 121

K

Kant, Immanuel, 94

L

law enforcement, 33
laws, 6, 8, 11, 17, 44, 46, 70, 86, 118, 125, 129
laws and regulations, 118
lawyers, 127
leadership, 3, 8, 9, 11, 13, 14, 15, 18, 19, 24, 25, 27, 29, 32, 38, 44, 48, 62, 63, 64, 70, 72, 78, 79, 84, 85, 87, 102
leadership development, 79
learning, 32, 76, 77, 80, 131
legal issues, 128
legality, 125
legislation, 122
life experiences, 33
lifelong learning, 79
light, 69, 128
low risk, 68
loyalty, 10, 13, 19, 24, 25, 33, 46, 48, 50, 72, 75, 97, 101, 102, 129

M

majority, 42, 89
maltreatment, 59, 67, 97

management, 10, 29, 39, 43, 51, 54, 59, 66, 78, 79, 97, 105, 130, 131
marriage, 124
Maryland, 90, 92
mass, 37, 51, 52, 65
materials, 90
matrix, 75, 114, 117, 126
matter, 2, 5, 36, 89, 90, 91, 92
Medicaid, 91
medical, vii, 1, 2, 3, 4, 5, 6, 7, 8, 9, 10, 11, 12, 13, 14, 15, 16, 17, 18, 19, 20, 21, 22, 23, 24, 26, 27, 28, 29, 30, 31, 32, 33, 35, 36, 37, 38, 39, 40, 41, 42, 43, 44, 45, 51, 52, 53, 54, 55, 56, 57, 58, 59, 60, 61, 62, 63, 64, 65, 66, 67, 68, 69, 70, 71, 72, 73, 75, 76, 77, 78, 79, 80, 81, 82, 83, 84, 85, 86, 87, 88, 89, 93, 95, 97, 98, 101, 106, 107, 109, 110, 111, 112, 113, 114, 115, 116, 117, 118, 120, 123, 124, 127, 128, 129, 130, 131
medical care, 35, 53, 59, 65, 77, 110, 111, 114, 131
medical reason, 65
Medicare, 91
medicine, vii, 10, 14, 23, 24, 29, 39, 52, 54, 62, 76, 77, 79, 102, 103, 107, 109, 110, 111, 112, 114, 117, 125, 127, 129
memory, 32
mental health, 13, 37, 40, 48, 56, 57, 58, 95
mental health professionals, 13, 48
mental illness, 38
mentoring, 16, 67, 106
methodology, 88
military, vii, 1, 2, 3, 4, 5, 6, 7, 8, 9, 10, 11, 12, 13, 14, 15, 16, 17, 18, 19, 20, 21, 22, 23, 24, 25, 26, 27, 28, 29, 31, 32, 33, 37, 38, 42, 43, 44, 45, 46, 47, 48, 49, 52, 53, 54, 55, 56, 57, 59, 61, 62, 63, 64, 66, 67, 69, 70, 71, 72, 73, 75, 76, 77, 79, 80, 81, 83, 84, 85, 86, 87, 88, 89, 101, 102, 104, 107, 109, 110, 111, 112, 113, 114, 115, 116, 117, 118, 119, 120, 121, 122, 123, 124, 125, 127, 128, 129, 130, 131, 133
military exercises, 77
military pressure, 112

mission(s), vii, 3, 5, 13, 14, 15, 16, 25, 32, 48, 51, 52, 53, 54, 56, 57, 62, 63, 67, 68, 69, 75, 77, 78, 79, 84, 107, 109, 111, 112, 113, 114, 115, 116, 117, 119, 120, 123, 124, 125, 130
misuse, 114, 123
mitochondria, 122
mitochondrial DNA, 122
modules, 76
molecules, 107
moral beliefs, 4, 8, 11, 32, 44, 87
moral judgment, 121
moral standards, 129
morale, 8, 11, 32, 44, 87
morality, 3, 24

N

naming, 127
National Defense Authorization Act, 132
national origin, 35
national security, 38, 85, 103
nationality, 36, 57
natural disaster(s), vii, 3, 15, 62, 66
neglect, 67
Netherlands, 101
nurses, 35, 39, 65, 75, 106
nursing, 24, 75, 78, 79
nutrition, 96

O

obedience, 13, 48, 112, 131
objectivity, 119
officials, 33
omission, 32, 47
operations, 2, 3, 4, 5, 8, 9, 11, 13, 15, 16, 18, 19, 21, 25, 26, 27, 28, 44, 52, 53, 54, 55, 57, 58, 59, 61, 62, 67, 68, 70, 72, 81, 83, 84, 86, 87, 89, 105
opportunities, 18, 20, 28, 72, 79, 82, 98, 114
organs, 28
outpatient, 76
oversight, 9, 10, 27, 33, 122

ovum, 122

P

pain, 77, 118
parents, 94
participants, 84
patient care, 18, 35, 43, 69, 70, 78, 127
peace, 15, 28, 36, 67
permit, 8, 11, 38, 44, 86
Persian Gulf, 118, 119, 131
Persian Gulf War, 118, 119
personal values, 11, 43
physical abuse, 33
physicians, 14, 28, 36, 37, 38, 62, 66, 78, 81, 82, 95, 96, 97, 98, 101, 102, 105, 109, 110, 111, 112, 114, 115, 116, 117, 118, 119, 120, 121, 125, 127, 128, 129, 130, 131
policy, 9, 10, 13, 17, 27, 34, 38, 39, 48, 58, 64, 69, 78, 94, 110, 114, 115, 117, 118, 119, 122, 123, 124, 127, 130
policy makers, 110, 115, 117, 122, 130
pollution, 54
population, 34, 54, 59, 62, 67, 78, 120
post-traumatic stress disorder (PTSD), 63, 102
potential benefits, 31
power inequality, 117
precedent, 127
prejudice, 34
preparation, 9, 22, 27, 84
preparedness, 37
preservation, 52
President, 2, 92, 105
prevention, 14, 63, 133
principles, vii, 5, 7, 9, 10, 17, 21, 22, 27, 28, 29, 30, 31, 32, 33, 34, 37, 40, 47, 57, 70, 73, 75, 76, 77, 78, 80, 84, 86, 95, 97, 109
prisoners, 29, 37, 51, 53, 57, 69, 80, 95, 96, 120, 131
prisoners of war, 51, 57, 80, 120, 131
prisons, 39, 96
privation, 54
professional development, 9, 27, 85

professionalism, 46, 107
professionals, vii, 2, 3, 4, 5, 6, 7, 8, 9, 10, 11, 13, 14, 15, 16, 17, 18, 19, 20, 21, 23, 24, 25, 26, 27, 28, 31, 34, 39, 41, 42, 44, 46, 49, 55, 56, 58, 63, 65, 67, 68, 69, 71, 72, 73, 75, 76, 79, 82, 83, 84, 85, 86, 87, 88, 89, 101
program staff, 43
prophylactic, 49, 118, 119, 120, 121
prophylactic agents, 118, 119, 120, 121
protection, 13, 26, 29, 36, 54, 57, 60, 95, 116, 120, 122, 127
psychiatry, 34
psychological health, 14, 63
psychology, 78
public health, vii, 3, 24, 33, 53, 54, 61, 74, 75, 77, 106, 131
punishment, 38, 57, 58, 95

Q

qualifications, 42
quality assurance, 123
quality control, 67
quality improvement, 43
quality of life, 81
quantification, 76
questioning, 121

R

race, 35, 36
reactions, 131
reading, 77, 107
reality, 73, 79, 111, 119
reasoning, 73, 78
recognition, 21, 52, 61, 71, 83
recombinant DNA, 29
recommendations, 1, 5, 6, 9, 22, 27, 28, 30, 42, 48, 57, 60, 78, 85, 88, 89, 117, 128
regulations, 13, 49
regulatory requirements, 10, 34
relatives, 98
relevance, 34, 60, 76

relief, 15, 66
religion, 48
religious beliefs, 6, 32, 88
repair, 32, 102
reproduction, 77
requirement(s), 6, 11, 13, 15, 20, 43, 48, 49, 52, 58, 59, 64, 69, 76, 80, 82, 83, 107, 111, 125, 127
resilience, 33
resistance, 37, 51
resolution, 6, 8, 20, 74, 82, 87, 94, 98, 107
resources, 5, 6, 7, 15, 16, 17, 21, 22, 29, 32, 34, 45, 51, 52, 54, 61, 64, 65, 68, 70, 76, 83, 84, 86
response, 4, 5, 9, 10, 13, 27, 29, 33, 38, 41, 52, 54, 58, 75, 84, 106, 119, 132
restrictions, 18, 28, 70
rights, 12, 30, 34, 39, 40, 45, 56, 69, 74, 98
risk(s), 23, 24, 30, 31, 32, 36, 49, 54, 56, 75, 96, 115, 116, 117, 118, 119, 120, 121, 122, 123, 124, 125, 129
risk assessment, 54
risk factors, 121
risk management, 56, 75
rules, 3, 13, 16, 24, 32, 47, 49, 50, 68, 75, 94

S

safety, 24, 26, 35, 57, 95, 111, 119
sanctions, 120
scarce resources, 3, 15, 24, 26
scholarship, 42
school, 75, 76, 77, 78, 80, 106, 107
science, 10, 23, 24, 29
scope, 4, 68, 88
Secretary of Defense, 1, 4, 38, 85, 88, 90, 98, 99, 103, 104, 122, 132
security, 54, 84, 122
self-sufficiency, 54
Senate, 103
sensitivity, 76
sentencing, 39
September 11, 119

services, vii, 2, 9, 12, 15, 27, 28, 35, 39, 40, 41, 42, 43, 44, 45, 53, 55, 56, 60, 61, 64, 96, 123, 132
sex, 35
sexual orientation, 35, 36
shame, 32
short supply, 24
siblings, 123
side effects, 31
simulations, 21, 83
skeletal remains, 131
smallpox, 120, 131
smoking, 120
social justice, 78
social standing, 36
social workers, 106
society, 10, 23, 28, 34, 46, 48, 78, 94, 109, 110, 111, 112, 113, 115, 116, 119, 120, 129, 130
solution, 114
South Africa, 96, 101
Spain, 96
specialists, 53, 55, 59, 65
specter, 52
Spring, 101
stability, 53, 77
stabilization, 13, 51, 53
staffing, 71, 77
stakeholders, 41
standardization, 76
state(s), 20, 23, 34, 35, 37, 38, 39, 40, 42, 47, 52, 53, 55, 57, 58, 59, 61, 65, 66, 74, 76, 107, 124, 127
statutes, 36
statutory authority, 111, 115
stethoscope, 112
stress, 13, 15, 18, 26, 29, 48, 54, 64, 71, 124
stressors, 16, 68
structure, 3, 25
structuring, 74
substance abuse, 56
suicide, 14, 58, 63
supervisor(s), 56
Supreme Court, 41
surrogates, 41

survival, 51, 115, 116
survivors, 61
Switzerland, 105
symptoms, 119
syndrome, 119, 131

T

target, 71
target population, 71
Task Force, 58, 105
teams, 26, 41, 52
techniques, 38
technological advances, 10, 28, 33
technolog(ies), 114, 122
tension(s), 3, 25, 63, 110, 129
term plans, 53
terminally ill, 31
territory, 3, 25, 120
terrorism, 105
terrorist attack(s), 119
textbook, 75
therapeutic relationship, 14, 62
therapy, 97, 128
threats, 26, 97, 120
torture, 10, 32, 37, 38, 60, 95, 96
toxin, 120
traditions, 47, 127
training, vii, 2, 3, 5, 7, 9, 12, 13, 14, 16, 17, 19, 20, 21, 22, 27, 32, 42, 44, 45, 46, 50, 51, 58, 61, 62, 64, 66, 68, 69, 70, 71, 72, 73, 75, 76, 79, 80, 81, 82, 83, 84, 85, 86, 89, 112, 113
training programs, 9, 19, 22, 27, 72, 75
transactions, 56
transformation, 10, 33
transgression, 4, 32, 33
transparency, 85
transportation, 59
trauma, 51, 53, 66
treaties, 47, 60
treatment, vii, 3, 10, 12, 13, 14, 15, 16, 24, 26, 27, 28, 31, 32, 33, 36, 37, 38, 39, 42, 45, 51, 53, 54, 56, 57, 58, 59, 60, 61, 63, 64, 65, 66, 68, 69, 77, 80, 81, 95, 97, 111, 113, 116, 128
trial, 37, 128
tuberculosis, 33

U

uniform, 76, 111, 112
United Kingdom, 92
United Nations, 55, 94, 107
United States, vii, 3, 9, 23, 27, 47, 48, 54, 61, 67, 84, 98, 99, 103, 104, 105, 106, 111, 122, 129, 132

V

vaccinations, 48
vaccine, 49, 119, 121, 131, 132
validation, 105
variations, 16, 67
victims, 54, 96
Vietnam, 122, 131
violence, 33, 36, 131
virus infection, 131
viruses, 131
vision, 117
volatility, 26
vote, 89
vulnerability, 112, 113
vulnerable people, 97

W

war, 9, 15, 27, 32, 52, 66, 84, 99, 101, 102, 105, 119, 121, 123
Washington, 93, 101, 102, 103, 104, 105, 106, 132
waste, 47, 79
water, 54
weapons, 49, 53, 66, 121
wcb, 79
welfare, 13, 30, 48, 59, 97, 103
well-being, 71, 74, 120
West Africa, 67, 106

White House, 49, 106
work environment, 28
World Health Organization, 76, 106
World War I, 60, 129
worldwide, 61, 62

Yale University, 102